The
Beginnings of
American
Methodism

JOHN O. GROSS

The
Beginnings of
American
Methodism

ABINGDON PRESS   NEW YORK — NASHVILLE

THE BEGINNINGS OF AMERICAN METHODISM

Copyright © 1961 by Abingdon Press

Library of Congress Catalog Card Number: 61-5193

SET UP, PRINTED, AND BOUND BY THE
PARTHENON PRESS, AT NASHVILLE,
TENNESSEE, UNITED STATES OF AMERICA

PREFACE

The purpose of the volume is to present a brief survey of the first years of The Methodist Church in the United States. Obviously there is much important material that could not be included—space would not permit it. I will know that my mission has been accomplished, however, if this book gives to Methodists of today a greater understanding of the heritage of their church and stimulates in them a desire to learn more about the persons "who fought a wilderness to found . . . Thy holy church on high and holy ground."

This volume grew out of a series of lessons prepared for the *Adult Student* (July-August, 1959) on early Methodist history in the United States. While this series served a special need at a special time, it was completely reorganized and rewritten to carry the story of our church's beginnings in the United States.

Like all who have written in the field of Methodist history, I am indebted to many persons for help in preparing this book. The large number of references made to books covering the period of Methodist beginnings will indicate my obligation to other writers. I am deeply grateful to Dr. Charles M. Laymon and his connection with the book through the writing assignment for the *Adult Student;* to Dr. Woodrow A. Geier, my associate, and to Bishop James W. Henley for their candid criticisms; and to Miss Marie Pomeranz, my administrative assistant, for her patience in caring for the many details necessary to prepare this book for publication.

CONTENTS

CHAPTER I

John Wesley's Search
for Religious Assurance

ALONG WITH OTHER METHODISTS THROUGHOUT THE world, American Methodists trace the beginning of their church to a house in Aldersgate Street, London. This building no longer stands, but a bronze plaque marks the site where, on May 24, 1738, John Wesley's heart was "strangely warmed." While Wesley's conversion occurred in a humble Moravian prayer meeting attended by only a few persons, it was a significant event in the history of the Christian church.

What happened at Aldersgate was an event in a chain reaction set off by Paul in his discussion of Christian faith in his letter to the Romans. During the reading of Martin Luther's interpretation of Paul's description of the change which God works in the heart through faith in Christ, John Wesley felt his heart strangely warmed. He said, "I felt I did trust in Christ, Christ alone for salvation: And an assurance was given me, that he had taken away my sins, even *mine* and saved *me* from the law of sin and death." [1]

Wesley's experience corresponds to the description of conversion given by William James: "To be converted, to be regenerated, to receive grace, to experience religion, to gain an assurance . . . denote the process, gradual or sudden, by which a self hitherto divided, and consciously wrong inferior and un-

---

[1] *Works of John Wesley,* I, 103.

happy, becomes unified and consciously right superior and happy, in consequence of its firmer hold upon religious realities." [2]

Psychologists recognize that an idea deposited in the mind goes through a period of growth before it reaches fruition. Wesley's conversion illustrates this fact. His Aldersgate experience does not stand as an isolated event. To understand what happened at Aldersgate, it is necessary to review the story of Wesley's life before Aldersgate.

For most of this thirty-five years before Aldersgate Wesley lived an acceptable religious life. His life forms one of the best-known case studies on religious nurture and growth available. His father, the Rev. Samuel Wesley, was the rector of the established church (Church of England) at Epworth. Fitchett calls him a "little, restless-eyed, irascible man; high-minded, quick-brained, . . . but with an impracticable, not to say irresponsible, strain in his blood." [3] Susannah Wesley, his mother, brought to the Wesley rectory the understanding of practical affairs which was missing in her husband's life. Withal, she can be called one of the world's great mothers. She was highly intelligent and very independent. Once she confided to John, "It is a misfortune almost peculiar to our family that your father and I seldom think alike." [4] This could also have been said of her relationship to her own father. At thirteen years of age she decided that the theological doctrines of his church were not correct. Then she forthwith withdrew from it and joined the established church.

Susannah Wesley had acquired a broad education, something unusual for a woman in her day. She determined that all her

[2] William James, *The Varieties of Religious Experience* (New York: Longmans, Green & Company, 1902), p. 189.

[3] W. F. Fitchett, *Wesley and His Century* (Cincinnati: The Abingdon Press, 1917), p. 23.

[4] *Ibid*, p. 24.

12

children would be educated. Her system of training began in the nursery where the children were required to cry softly. John was taught early to distinguish the Sabbath from other days, to ask the blessing at meals by signs before he could kneel or speak, to be still at family prayers, and to repeat the Lord's prayer. His formal training began at five in his own household with his mother as teacher. One day only was allowed for learning the alphabet. This training plan included an hour once a week with her in private conversation on the beliefs taught by the church.

His understanding of the requirements of the church justified his father's admitting him to the Lord's Supper at eight years of age. The dramatic rescue of John Wesley from the fire which destroyed the Epworth parsonage indicated to his parents that he had been providentially spared for some unusual purpose. A record made by his mother when he was fourteen indicated that she believed he was destined to fill an important place in life. She then resolved to be more particularly careful with the soul of the boy, whom God had provided for, so that she might "instill into his mind the principles of true religion and virtue."

At ten John's education had advanced sufficiently under his mother's tutelage to qualify him for admission to one of England's famous schools, Charterhouse. Here his name was linked to a roster of distinguished alumni—Addison, Steele, Blackstone, Roger Williams—to mention only a few. Charterhouse was not only a period in his educational life but also one in his religious life. In the radical change from the pious, sheltered rectory to an eighteenth-century boys' school, Tyerman says, Wesley lost the religion which had marked his character from the days of infancy! "John Wesley entered the Charterhouse a saint, and left it a sinner." [5]

---

[5] Tyerman, *Life and Times of Wesley* (New York: Harper & Brothers, 1872), I, 21 ff.

At seventeen, Wesley enrolled at Christ College, Oxford. He remained at Oxford as an undergraduate student and as a teacher for almost fifteen years. During his student days, he maintained a high scholastic record, but his interest in religious matters was, to say the least, only nominal.

Because of John Wesley's connection with Oxford, Methodists sometimes speak of it as the cradle of their church. Oxford, itself, however, was not the source of Methodist evangelical fervor. While the name Methodist originated there, it was given to an "extracurricular" group known as the "Holy Club," which had been organized by John's brother, Charles. The club met for prayer and Bible study. It encouraged its members to fast and to labor among the poor. John Wesley became a zealous member of this club. Through it, he earnestly sought to satisfy his spiritual hungers by meticulously following the rules of the church.

The austere discipline and systematic planning adopted by these young men at Oxford became permanent habits in their lives. Here John Wesley learned to deprive himself of all things bordering on luxury. He confined his wants to the necessities. From this time throughout his entire life the practices of self-denial formed there were conscientiously followed. He enjoined this austerity upon others as basic for spiritual growth. For example, as a student in Oxford, when he had an income of 30 pounds a year, he lived on 28 and gave away the difference. When he was made a fellow (a tutor) and his income reached 120 pounds, he continued to live on 28 and gave the balance to the poor. This may explain why he was able during his lifetime to give away between 20,000 and 30,000 pounds. Once he declared that his own hands should be his executors, and that if he died with more than 10 pounds, independent of his books, the world could call him a "thief and a robber."

The religion of John Wesley as a member of the Holy Club has been described by W. H. Fitchett as one with a high-church flavor! "It utterly lacked the element of joy. Religion is meant to have for the spiritual landscape the office of sunshine, but in Wesley's spiritual sky burned no divine light, whether of certainty or hope. He imagined he could distill the rich wine of spiritual gladness out of mechanical religious exercises." [6] Wesley ended his days at Oxford without having attained an awareness of being accepted by God or with any satisfying sense of religious certainty. This is his estimate of the value of the Holy Club:

Yet when, after continuing for some years in this course, [the practices of the Holy Club] I apprehended myself to be near death, I could not find that all this gave me any comfort or any assurance of acceptance with God. At this I was then not a little surprised; not imagining I had been all this time building on sand, nor considering that "other foundation can no man lay than that which is laid" by God "even Jesus Christ." [7]

Wesley became a priest in the Church of England in 1728. For about two years he served as his father's curate (the name for an assistant) at Epworth and Wroote. He had been well prepared for the work in his studies of theology. He had a trained and disciplined mind. His zeal and energy were tireless. Despite his discipline and zeal, however, the two years he served as a parish priest were disappointing to himself and to the people. This is how he summed up his labors:

I preached much, but saw no fruit of my labour. Indeed, it could not be that I should, for I neither laid the foundation of repentance

[6] *Op. cit.,* p. 84.
[7] *John Wesley's Journal,* May, 1738, I, 100.

nor of believing the Gospel, taking it for granted that all to whom I preached were believers, and that many of them needed no repentance.[8]

The road to Aldersgate was a long and circuitous one. In 1735, John Wesley sailed for Georgia where he was to spend two and a half years as missionary to the Indians and minister to the settlers. True holiness, Wesley the ascetic believed, could be reached mainly through suffering and rigid self-discipline. Georgia surely could furnish the hardships requiring personal denial. On October 10, 1735, three days before leaving for Georgia, he had recorded his purpose: "My chief motive is the hope of saving my own soul. I hope to learn the true sense of the Gospel of Christ by preaching it to the heathen." [9]

Methodists of America sometimes link the mission of John Wesley to Georgia with the beginnings of their church. The Wesley that Georgia knew, however, was not a Methodist but a sacerdotal ecclesiastic. Some of his hearers, greatly puzzled by his preaching and ritualism, could not decide whether he was a Protestant or a Roman Catholic. All the time he was there, he sought to establish his own righteousness through enforcing an intolerant and rigid system of legalistic disciplines upon an ignorant and unwilling people.

Wesley's ministry in Georgia, like his previous service at Wroote, was empty of vital spiritual power. Governor James Oglethorpe observed that there was "no true religion amongst the people; but instead of this, mere formal prayers." Robert Southey blamed Wesley's failure upon his inability to recognize his parishioners as babes and feed them on milk. "Instead of this he drenched them with the physic of an intolerant discipline." [10]

[8] Fitchett, *op. cit.,* 74.
[9] Tyerman, *op. cit.,* I, 115.
[10] *Life of Wesley* (New York: Oxford University Press), I, 67.

Wesley's experiences in Georgia hastened the maturing processes which were to flower at Aldersgate. Chief among these was the acquaintance with the Moravians, who were to lead him out of his religious wilderness. These people were religious refugees who had been driven from Moravia by the persecution of the Jesuits and had settled in Herrnhut, Germany. Wesley noticed during a storm that threatened the ship that the Moravians remained calm and serene while the English aboard trembled and screamed hysterically. Here he saw the difference in the time of testing between Christians who feared God and those who did not.

The religion that the Moravians exemplified intrigued Wesley. He studied German in order to talk with them about their faith. Their pastor, August Gottlieb Spangenberg, was a scholar from the University of Jena, but nevertheless a humble man whose chief aim was to bring men into a living relationship with Jesus Christ. When the ship landed, Wesley went to Spangenberg for counsel with regard to his personal religious life. Spangenberg replied: "My brother, I must first ask you one or two questions. Have you the witness within yourself? Does the Spirit of God bear witness with your spirit, that you are a child of God?" [11] Wesley found these searching questions disquieting. He could answer only with wide generalizations.

A series of unpleasant experiences, some romantic in nature, but all tied to the grievances made by his rigid ecclesiasticism, led to his departure from Georgia. His ministry, though, was not a failure. Wesley's experiences in Georgia, on the whole, as the late H. B. Workman has said, "did much to mould the character of the man. . . . It prepared the way for a theology pene-

---

[11] Tyerman, *op. cit.*, I, 125.

trated with the light of evangelical mysticism, and broad as the charity of God." [12]

The years in Georgia cannot be charged off as entirely barren. Space is too limited to cover the many constructive by-products of his ministry, such as the translation of German hymns and the publication of a "Collection of Psalms and Hymns." He also translated the "writings of holy men in the German, Spanish, and Italian tongues." [13]

The forty-day return voyage from Georgia to England gave Wesley time for introspection and soul searching. He had tested his religion. He found it wanting: "I went to America to convert the Indians; but oh, who shall convert me? I have a fair summer religion." [14] Disillusioned by the two years of fruitless effort, he saw that a formal acceptance of the truths of Christianity, along with a dedication that sent him to live in a strange land, had not brought forgiveness of sins and reconciliation with God. But this entry in his journal on the day he landed in England shows that his face was toward the light: "I have no hope, but if I seek I shall find Christ and be found in him, not having my own righteousness, but that which is through the faith of Christ, the righteousness which is of God by faith."

After reaching England, Wesley promptly reported to the authorities on the Georgia settlement. Then he turned to what he regarded as his most pressing need—namely, to possess a sure trust and confidence in God, and to know that he was reconciled to God.

On February 7, 1738, six days after landing in England, he

[12] W. J. Townsend, H. B. Workman, and George Eayrs, *A New History of Methodism* (Nashville: Publishing House of The Methodist Episcopal Church, South, 1909, out of print), I, 195.

[13] Wesley, *Journal.*

[14] Tyerman, *op. cit.,* I, 166.

met the man who was to be the Ananias to help him find his spiritual sight. Peter Bohler, a twenty-five-year-old Moravian, diagnosed Wesley as a "man of good principles, who knew he did not properly believe on the Savior and was willing to be taught." Bohler found that while Wesley was receptive to instruction, he had to be convinced that the Moravian idea of redemption was based upon the teachings of the Bible. During this time Bohler noted that the Moravian approach to salvation "of believing in the Savior seems so easy to Englishmen that they cannot reconcile themselves to it. If it were a little more difficult, they would much sooner find their way into it. They take it for granted that they believe already, and try to prove their faith by their works, and thus so torment themselves that they are at heart very miserable." Bohler supplemented his arguments by personal witnesses who testified of their joy in Christ.

During this period of serious search, Wesley felt that he should give up preaching salvation by faith since he did not have the assurance of it in his own life. But Bohler told him to keep on preaching until he personally had the experience. This he did, so that a prisoner who had been condemned to die accepted Christ at Wesley's urging and went to the scaffold with a "sincere peace." After several weeks under Bohler, Wesley wrote, "I see the promise; but it is afar off." [15]

Wesley's crisis on May 24, 1738, was preceded by some encouraging signs. At 5 A.M. he opened his Greek Testament and read, "[There] are given unto us exceeding great and precious promises: even that . . . ye might be partakers of the divine nature." (II Pet. 1:4.) This assured him that he could be renewed in the divine image so that God could dwell in him. Later, while worshiping at St. Paul's Cathedral, the anthem, "Out of

---

[15] Holland N. McTyeire, *A History of Methodism* (Nashville: Southern Methodist Publishing House, 1884), p. 115.

the deep have I called unto Thee, O Lord, hear my voice," expressed the cry of his own soul.

Yet with all these favorable signs, Wesley "went very unwillingly" that evening to the Moravian meeting in Aldersgate Street. There a printer named William Holland read an interpretation of salvation by faith from Martin Luther's Preface to the Epistle to the Romans. Here are the words from Luther at the Aldersgate Street meeting:

Faith is an energy in the heart, so efficacious, lively, breathing, powerful as to be incapable of remaining inactive. Faith is a constant trust in the mercy of God toward us, by which we cast ourselves entirely on Christ and commit ourselves entirely to him. . . . This firm trust is so animating as to cheer and elevate the heart and transport it with affections toward God. The believer feels no dread in opposing himself as a single champion against all creatures. The high and heroic feeling, this noble enlargement of the spirit is effected in the heart by the spirit of God, who is imparted to the believers by faith. It is impossible to separate works from faith, as impossible as to sever light from the heat in the fire.

Aldersgate linked the Methodist revival with the Protestant Reformation. Luther here, as Workman points out, focused Wesley's "attention on the nature of faith as 'a vital energy in our hearts,' and upon the living object of faith." [16]

No language can adequately describe what happens when God reveals himself to man. God transformed Wesley's life at Aldersgate. Here he got a firm hold on religious realities and became "consciously right superior and happy." He immediately left the room on Aldersgate Street and "was brought in triumph by a troop of friends to a house" in Little Britain where his

[16] Townsend, Workman, and Eayrs, op. cit., p. 201.

brother Charles was confined with pleurisy. He saluted Charles with *"I believe."* The day before, Charles waked, as he said, "under the protection of Christ and gave myself up, soul and body, to Him." [17] With the new experience on that same day came this hymn from Charles's pen:

> Where shall my wondering soul begin?
> How shall I all to heaven aspire?
> A slave redeemed from death and sin,
> A brand plucked from eternal fire,
> How shall I equal triumphs raise,
> Or sing my great Deliverer's praise?

There, about 10 P.M., the Wesley brothers and their friends sang this hymn together. Something had happened to both.

Without question, Wesley's experience marked a turning point in his career. John Wesley, the man with a richly endowed mind, broad scholarship, and culture, a stickler for orderliness and decency in worship, became a new Wesley who from this time was unconventional, a companion and associate of humble souls, and a zealous evangelist.

At Aldersgate Wesley placed faith before works as a means of salvation. He turned away from some of the thought patterns and religious practices in which he had been nurtured from childhood. This started, said William Sargant, English psychiatrist, a total reorientation of his religious position, one as radical as the change from political conservatism to communism would be today." [18]

Had John Wesley been a Christian before Aldersgate? A sympathetic Anglican biographer, Canon Overton, thought that

---

[17] Leslie F. Church, *Knight of the Burning Heart* (Nashville: Abingdon Press, 1953), p. 94.
[18] *Battle for the Mind* (New York: Doubleday & Company, 1957), p. 96.

Wesley's disclaim of being a Christian prior to Aldersgate was extravagant, and said that if John Wesley was not a true Christian when in Georgia, "God help all those who profess and call themselves Christians." [19] Five days after Aldersgate, Wesley said that he had never been a Christian. He told a small group that the only way possible for them to become Christians was to believe and confess that they were not so now. This occurred, Southey notes, while he was in a "delirious stage of enthusiasm." A Mrs. Hutton who heard him sharply rebuked him: "If you were not a Christian ever since I knew you, you was a great hypocrite, for you made us all believe you were one." [20]

Wesley, himself, in later years recognized that Aldersgate marked an epoch in his life, but that it was neither the beginning nor the end of his Christian life. Here, Umphrey Lee says:

Wesley had reached the stage when all his energies and interests were channeled into his devotion to God. His conversion, in short, was not an evangelical but a mystical conversion—that is, the conversion of a religious man to a higher state of religious devotion. . . . His strangely warmed heart signifies what Piette calls an "intense perception of the love of God." And this perception of the love of God awoke in him an answering love.[21]

We know now that Methodist teaching concerning the new birth goes beyond Aldersgate. Then, in the intensity of the afterglow of his religious experience, Wesley made some dogmatic statements about the way God's spirit works that later were modified. In a letter to Melville Horne he said:

When fifty years ago my brother and I, in the simplicity of our hearts, told the good people of England that unless they knew their

[19] Fitchett, *op. cit.*, p. 127.
[20] Southey, *op. cit.*, p. 120-21.
[21] *John Wesley and Modern Religion* (Nashville: Cokesbury Press, 1936), p. 103-4.

22

sins were forgiven, they were under the wrath and curse of God, I marvel, Melville, that they did not stone us! The Methodists, I hope, know better now; we preach assurance as we always did, as a common privilege of the children of God, but we do not enforce it under the pain of damnation, denounced on all who enjoy it not.[22]

From Aldersgate on, Wesley did hold that it was possible for one to possess the consciousness of being in the favor of God. This consciousness he held up as a common privilege of Christians. Yet he admitted exceptions to the rule, these being necessary, he said, either "to disorder of body or ignorance of the gospel promises." [23] As his thoughts on Aldersgate matured, he concluded that there he was made a child of God. Previously he had been only a servant.

Increasingly Wesley saw that Aldersgate stood for spiritual emancipation. It was there that his inner tensions, apprehensions, and doubt had given way to peace, truth, and certainty. By following the leading of God's spirit, he became a member of the family of God and entered into the liberty of a child of God. Freed from the attributes of a slave, he was released from the slavish attitudes which had dominated his life.

The warning drawn from Wesley's life for all of us is that living doctrines may become empty, meaningless words. Wesley's work at Oxford gave to him an intellectual understanding of the nature of Christianity. But the doctrines for him were "a set of pale and colourless syllables out of which all reality had drained. . . . His experience proves afresh that a creed may survive as a bit of literature; it may be chanted in hymns, and woven into prayers and solemnly taught as a theology, and yet be exhausted of all life." [24]

[22] *Sermons*, I, 82, f.n.
[23] *Letters*, V, 358-9.
[24] Fitchett, *op. cit.*, p. 128.

A writer on American Methodism reports a conversation between Francis Asbury and Jesse Lee in February, 1785, while the two were on a journey through North Carolina. Asbury said:

> I have been meditating on our mission to Charleston. We are going to attempt to introduce Methodism into that city. Fifty years ago, Mr. Wesley went there, and to the adjoining city, Savannah, a missionary from beyond the sea; but his mission failed, and he returned home discouraged, as much dissatisfied with his own religious state as with the failure of his mission. Why do we hope to succeed? Is it not because we go to tell them of a religion that has affected our own hearts; that we have felt and seen? Wesley could not do this. . . . He came, a Christian Pharisee, to convert men to the observance of rituals and forms: we go to declare the efficacy of salvation by faith in Christ, and the blessed assurance that every man may have of it by the Holy Ghost. What a lesson his failure teaches us!—what else, than that every effort to save men but by faith will always be a failure? [25]

Asbury's analysis indicates that Wesley's significant contribution to religion came out of his evangelical experience. From Aldersgate forward, Wesley's constant emphasis was upon the spiritual power released through the power of faith. The values of the Christian faith must be conferred by the spirit of God. Above everything else, Wesley wanted Methodists to possess a living relationship with God. This relationship, he held, was the only way to prevent Methodists from existing as a "dead sect having the form of religion without the power."

[25] M. L. Scudder, *American Methodism* (Hartford, Conn.: S. S. Scranton & Co., 1876, out of print), p. 269-70.

CHAPTER II

Forward From Aldersgate

ALDERSGATE WAS FOLLOWED BY A PERIOD OF RETIREMENT for meditation and readjustment. During that time Wesley continued to study Moravian beliefs and practices. In order to know them firsthand, he visited the Moravian settlement at Herrnhut, Germany. Here he was impressed by the Moravians' "love of the Blessed Redeemer, [their] deadness to the world, [their] meekness, temperance, chastity, and love of one another." [1] He left Germany with many apprehensions, however. After a brief period of identification with the Moravians in London, Wesley was drawn toward the work with which he would be identified for the next fifty years. The new liberty found at Aldersgate had released him not only from the legalism of the Church of England, but also from the exclusiveness and quietism of the Moravians. Now, after Aldersgate, as Bishop McConnell wrote, "His eyes were turned outward instead of inward." [2]

An understanding of the rise of Methodism in America requires some knowledge of the historical essentials and cultural facts which form the background of the work Wesley did in England. Here, we must remember, the first Methodist efforts in America were definitely a part of English Methodism and were directed from England by John Wesley himself. (There was definite kinship between the religious ideas of Methodists in both countries.) At the close of the Revolutionary War when

---

[1] Wesley, *Works*, VIII, 365.
[2] Francis J. McConnell, *John Wesley* (Nashville: Abingdon Press, 1939), p. 71.

separation became inevitable, John Wesley made plans for the new church.

Under Wesley the Methodist movement created a desire in England for improvement of moral, mental, and social life. It fostered a concern for education, prison reform, temperance, factory legislation, and freedom for the slaves. Without question, its effect upon the life of the English-speaking peoples was greater than that of any religious revival in their history. To appreciate the extent of the Wesleyan influence, we need a brief sketch of the moral life of England during the eighteenth century.

That period called for a leader who could bring deliverance and light. John Wesley proved to be the man. Wesley's newly found faith prepared him for his task. It is doubtful that apart from the Aldersgate experience he would have tried to meet the challenge. After it, like Cromwell in his day, Wesley believed that in Christ he would have strength for the era of reform England must undergo.

The England that John Wesley knew in the eighteenth century was one of transition. Its problems were associated with industrialization and its attendant counterpart, secularization. Lawlessness, irreligion, drunkenness, gambling, coarseness, and vulgarity were widespread. Reaction had set in against the austere morality imposed by the Puritans. These people, dedicated and zealous, believed legislation could exterminate vice and create righteousness. Anti-Puritans replied by encouraging unbridled license. During this period the springs of social and religious idealism all but dried up.

The story of the wickedness of Wesley's century has been narrated by many writers of history. It was a period when noble ideals gave way to base ones. Sports were brutal, public life was corrupt, and vice stalked unashamed. Public dishonesty was a crying scandal. The prime minister, Sir Robert Walpole, declared that an enemy in the field might buy the country, for every member of the Commons had his price. Walpole himself did not introduce political corruption into England, but he did much toward systematizing it! He lent his name and influence to efforts to suppress religious enthusiasm and to secularize the church.

Intoxicating liquors and low morality usually go together, and in this period it was especially true. The eighteenth century was England's "Gin Age." Cheap, fiery, poisonous alcohol flowed freely. Many "aristocrats were sodden lumps of flesh preserved in alcohol." [3] Wesley said that gin sent more to the regions of death than the sword or the plague and was "the arch plague among his countrymen." Every sixth house in London was a grog shop. Gin was so cheap that retailers displayed signs: "Drunk for 1d; Dead Drunk 2d; Free Straw to Lie On." The passion for alcohol affected all classes.[4]

The drinking houses were gathering places for the worst characters—thieves, robbers, and prostitutes. Law enforcement broke down. Acts of violence and robbery were committed without fear of consequence. John Wesley's meetings often were broken up by mobs incited by strong drink. He classified drunkenness as one of the great evils of his day. He noted that its debasing influence was felt in all levels of society.

Private life was fouled at the home bases. The baptism registers in the parishes show illegitimacy widespread in the villages. Personal chastity was derided. In fact, things of shame or pride became so inverted that gentlemen of that day would blush when accused of living pure lives.

---

[3] J. H. Whiteley, *Wesley's England* (London: The Epworth Press, 1938), p. 29.
[4] J. Wesley Bready, *England Before and After Wesley* (London: Hodder and Stoughton Limited, 1938), pp. 145-50.

It has often been observed that religion always has the sort of clergymen that it deserves. As a class, clergymen of the eighteenth century were disliked and without social standing. Since the appointment of men to offices in the Church of England rested with politicians, clergymen were not averse to pulling strings to get their jobs. Macaulay, observing the state of the church, said that when political power of the Anglican hierarchy was at its height, national morality was at its lowest. Many drunken, lazy, and ignorant clergymen scandalized their profession. The court of George II, known for its immorality, had divines who treated his debased morals as virtues. Detailed descriptions of the shortcomings of the clergy of that day do no honor to the profession. These conditions are mentioned here merely to help us understand the reforms needed to make the church itself respectable in English life.

Religion, it may be inferred from the quality of its leaders, ignored many of the beliefs that affect human conscience. Good advice supplanted good news. Moral essays that did not produce transformation of character became the prevailing fashion in the pulpits.

Deism flourished. Appealing to reason alone, deism was soulless and skeptical. Reason was magnified, and man was not considered as an emotional, imaginative being. Deism derided divine revelation and insisted that the ideas implanted by the Creator in the human mind teach all that can be known. The Gospel narratives, said Thomas Woolston, a leading deist of that century, were "a tissue of absurdities. . . . With coarse wit and jibing satire, he sneered not only at the works and teaching, but also at the character, of Christ." [5] Deistic teaching was the religion of fashionable society, since it relaxed the bonds of morality and permitted greater license in conduct. Intellectualism

[5] *Ibid.*, p. 35.

by itself alone, the eighteenth century shows, cannot exert the influence required for Christian living.

The great universities of England which should have been lights in this dark age degenerated. Sound learning and serious education were not their special concerns. Men like Wesley and Gibbon got their education in spite of them. Gibbon spoke of the time he spent at Oxford "as fourteen idle and unprofitable months." [6] Professorships, like bishoprics, became political prizes, and academic honors could be bestowed without examinations upon students able to buy their degrees.

In this period few of the leaders presented any constructive plans for improving the lot of the uneducated, immoral, and ignorant populace. Members of Parliament did institute investigations, but like their counterparts in this century (congressional committees), their efforts to correct evils were feeble, if not futile. How was England to raise its debauched people? John Wesley had a practical and rational approach to it—a revitalizing of the Christian faith.

Under Wesley's leadership, Methodism became "Christianity in earnest." Wesley's break with the Moravians and their quietism opened the way for an era of active, aggressive Christianity. He was not constituted to sit still and do nothing in the presence of spiritual sterility. Wesley accepted the challenge of eighteenth-century England and formulated plans to meet it.

It is doubtful if John Wesley ever drew up a blueprint for the moral and spiritual rehabilitation of England. He took one step at a time and let his plans unfold as the battle developed. When a study is made of what he accomplished, however, one finds that the stratagem used to reach his goals was carefully thought out. In his period of orientation Wesley reviewed his study of the practices of the early church. He became convinced

[6] *Ibid.*, p. 54.

that nothing short of a vast mass movement back to the teachings of primitive Christianity could save England. Thus, he planned ways for instructing the ignorant, reforming the wicked, and maturing the awakened. He resolved to go directly to the people. This decision pushed him further away from his high-church convictions. It called for a change in the manner and place where he conducted public services.

Even after his conversion Wesley believed that to preach anywhere except from the pulpit of the established church was irreverent and impious. Soon, however, the pulpits of his church were increasingly closed to him. Even the pulpit in his father's church at Epworth was not open to him. His ardor and enthusiasm, plus his uncompromising opposition to the evils of his day, had made him unacceptable to the ecclesiastical leaders. But, armed with a "dispensation of the Gospel" under the urging of George Whitefield, a colleague of the Holy Club, he braved the opposition of his bishop and set up his pulpit in open market places and on the village greens.

In 1739 when a bishop ordered him to desist from open-air preaching, he justified his unprecedented departure in one of his most often quoted declarations: On July 11, 1739, he wrote in his journal, "I look upon all the world as my parish, thus far, I mean, that in whatever part of it I am I judge it meet, right, and my bounden duty to declare unto all that are willing to hear the glad tidings of salvation."

Thus the Wesleyan mass movement began. For the next fifty years Wesley and his dedicated preachers took the gospel to all England. The people who came to meetings for the most part consisted of society's outcasts—the poor, with a sprinkling of inebriates, thieves, prostitutes, and the degraded. To Wesley they were needy individuals beyond the reach of the church.

The Methodist movement quickly took hold in England. The

secret of its success is no mystery. John Wesley detected the latent spiritual hunger existing in his day and set himself to nourish the people with the gospel of Christ. In doing this he revived the basic Christian teachings which had been neglected, if not wholly abandoned.

The doctrines Wesley preached were the ones then regarded as essential for personal salvation—the depravity of human nature; the lost condition of every man; the vicarious atonement of Christ; the necessity of salvation, of a new birth, of faith, of the constant and sustaining influence of the Holy Spirit upon the believer's soul. None of these could be called new. They were the admitted tenets of Anglican theology. The difference between Wesley's preaching and that of most other clergy of his day was in his earnestness and the special emphasis that he gave. He clothed old beliefs with new authority and power.

The results which followed Wesley's preaching were phenomenal—so much so that we should know something of its nature. In preaching, his unusual mental gifts are demonstrated. The England that he knew did not have a standard English language. There were hundreds of dialects to which he had to adjust his preaching. This called for skill in writing his sermons in simple and terse language. It has been said that in order to have the necessary simplicity and directness, he would read his sermons to an old maidservant and cross out every phrase that she did not understand.[7]

Wesley was a persuasive preacher who did not believe a man could "be bullied into heaven." He avoided pious clichés and holy talk which really meant nothing to the majority of his hearers. Once he said, "I am sick of hearing some men preach Christ. Let but a pert, self-sufficient animal that hath neither sense nor grace bawl out something about Christ, or his blood, or justification by faith and his hearers cry out, 'What a fine gospel sermon!' " Simplicity and directness were the chief characteristics of John Wesley's sermons.

While Wesley's sermons, as one of his hearers reported, were quiet as a Quaker's and stately as the lectures of a professor, let no one conclude that they lacked directness when evil needed to be rebuked. The Duchess of Buckingham found it "highly offensive and insulting" to be told "that you have a heart as sinful as *the common wretches that crawl on the earth.*" [8] He denounced slavery as worst of all villainies. He placed slave merchants as "men-buyers" on a level with "men-stealers." War, he held, was a "reproach to all reason and humanity. When war breaks out, God's forgotten." Spirituous liquors were "liquid fire," and those who distilled them were guilty of driving "men to hell like sheep." The sale of liquor for revenue purposes was termed no more than "selling the flesh and blood" of one's countrymen.

It is the universal testimony of those who closely studied Wesley's conversions that the results were not momentary reforms but lasting ones. Wherever conversions took place they were followed by a signal decrease in the evils of drunkenness, profanity, unchastity, and coarseness. The Kingswood miners, long known as the lowest in vice and lawlessness, were changed into a quiet, orderly, excellent community.

All this meant that Wesley worked upon the conviction that a change in England's life called for transformed people. He probably would have agreed with Emerson that lasting reform depended upon the influence of private character. This conviction would take on wide significance in view of the debauchery found at all levels of life. Wesley's work aimed at helping the individual, no matter how depressed he might be, to realize his

[8] Bready, *op. cit.*, p. 212.

possibilities as a child of God. Since sinful living was the obvious deterrent, there had to be a release from its tyranny and a new spiritual motive implanted. In an age which put a low estimate on the worth of persons, Wesley lived and worked with the wicked, the vile, and the bestial. All had souls worth saving. Through his work many depressed persons rose from the sordidness of their surroundings to a higher level of life.

Henry Bett holds that Methodism literally

lifted multitudes from a life of ignorance and brutality, and . . . made them intelligent and responsible men; it gave them some interest in books and music, if only at first in religious books and sacred music. Many a man who would otherwise have been a mere brute was brought, first of all, to an experience of religion, and then led to study his Bible, and to read some of the books written by Wesley or recommended by him.[9]

Wesley's interest in personal growth prompted him to make available the best literature in cheap bindings. He encouraged education for the people who were deprived of it because of their social standing. When six of the students from Kingswood, a school he founded in 1748, were expelled from Oxford because they were sons of tradesmen—barbers, weavers, taphouse keepers, and the like—and for having too much religion, he vowed that he would have an educational program at Kingswood superior in some respects to any university he had seen at home or abroad. Wesley obviously was set against the rigid stratification of English society which made it difficult for a man to rise to a higher class from the class into which he was born.

Some persons viewing Wesley through twentieth-century lenses may conclude that he was not interested in social achieve-

[9] H. F. Mathews, *Methodism and the Education of the People* (London: The Epworth Press, 1949), p. 77.

ments but only in personal religion. No student of Wesley's ministry can deny that his approach was to the individual. Many social achievements in the life of England, however, may be traced to Wesley's work. Lecky, the historian of the eighteenth century, credits Wesley with saving England from the fate of the French Revolution. This claim may be extravagant. Differences do exist between English and French attitudes toward constituted authority. If, however, as Lecky said, there was in England a tendency toward rebellion and a desire for revolutionary change, an ameliorating influence did come through the Methodist movement, which brought stability. This, Bready says, was done by Wesley who by "initiating and directing a marvellous spiritual movement latent with moral imperative . . . opened the springs of human sympathy and understanding, which in turn inspired and nourished a glorious succession of social reforms." [10]

Wesley regarded social advance as a reliable test for the genuineness of a revival of religion. He once said, "Christianity is essentially a social religion; and . . . to turn it into a solitary religion, is indeed to destroy it." [11] The Methodist movement was creative, and many of the advances made in England's domestic and social life were inspired by it. It produced a number of influential social leaders who were to protect labor from the inhumane practices brought on by the Industrial Revolution.

The Methodist movement was not to be limited to the British Isles, however. Among the immigrants who settled in America were many of Wesley's converts. As we shall see later, these converts had become a formidable factor in the religious life of the new nation even before Wesley's death in 1791.

[10] *Op. cit.*, p. 252.
[11] *Works*, V, 296.

CHAPTER III

Methodism
Takes Root in America

ALL THE CHRISTIAN CHURCHES FOUNDED IN AMERICA before the Revolutionary War traced their beginnings to Europe. New England, with the exception of Rhode Island, had established a puritanical Congregationalism. Rhode Island, settled by Baptists, took a liberal position for that day and showed a hospitable attitude toward all forms of worship. The Quakers and the Presbyterians occupied New Jersey and Pennsylvania. Delaware, settled by Swedes, introduced Lutheranism. Maryland had a liberal charter but was founded by Roman Catholics. Virginia was peopled by supporters of the Church of England. Further south, in addition to the Anglicans, there were Huguenots, Moravians, and Presbyterians. The original Dutch settlers brought both Lutheran and Reformed churches to New Amsterdam. New York, after coming under British rule, gave the Church of England priority, yet it had representatives of nearly every Christian church. Of all the religious bodies established in America before the Revolution, the Methodist was the weakest, both in numbers and influence.

Methodist work in America began with religious societies such as the ones which existed in England. Membership in a society was not considered the same as church membership; therefore, membership in some other church, especially the Church of England, was common. The first societies had closer ties with the Anglican than with any other church. A few ministers of the

Church of England, among them the Reverend Devereux Jarrett in Virginia, co-operated with the Methodists.

Churches that had an educated ministry considered the Methodist societies a coarse, ranting sect. Their worshipers sang enthusiastically, shouted, clapped their hands, and enjoyed a high degree of freedom in their services.

Despite a haphazard beginning, the Methodist movement in America was, in time, to develop into a church with which democracy could live and grow. Before a century passed, the Methodists had become powerful enough in the life of the new republic to be the most effective force in establishing order on the expanding frontier.

The Methodist movement had been under way in England for almost thirty years before it formally took root in America. For three decades after Aldersgate, Wesley made no move to include America in his plans. Historians differ about the spot where Methodism began in America. Some say New York. Others hold it first took rootage in Maryland soil. We leave the matter of priority to the historians, trusting that sometime in the future the objectivity needed for a conclusive decision will be possible.

The evangelical movement antedates the formal organization of Methodist societies. This religious awakening led by John and Charles Wesley and George Whitefield, three members of the Methodist "Holy Club" of Oxford, stirred England during the eighteenth century. Many persons who had been converted under Methodist preachers in England and Ireland had migrated to the New World. Furthermore, George Whitefield, who preached between 1739 and 1770, helped prepare the way for the coming of Methodism in America. There is a record of his organizing a Methodist Society in Delaware in 1739.[1]

[1] Charles W. Flint, *Charles Wesley and His Colleagues* (Washington, D.C.: Public Affairs Press, 1957), p. 42.

Along with John and Charles Wesley, Whitefield formed "a great gospel triumvirate." He became the great evangelist of the new awakening. In fact, he may properly be called the father of mass evangelism. At the age of twenty-two he was drawing great crowds in London with his preaching. Perhaps Christendom has not produced a more effective preacher to the masses. It was he who broke the exclusion that the Church of England had placed upon Methodist meetings by preaching in the open air.

When the chancellor of the Church of England at Bristol notified Whitefield that preaching in the diocese of Bristol without a license was against canon law, the latter asked why another canon law which forbade clergymen to frequent taverns and play cards was not enforced! He was not overawed by this church dignitary. To the youthful Whitefield, the souls of men were of more value than the most venerable edicts of the church. Observing that Jesus "had a mountain for his pulpit and the heavens for a sounding board," he took to the open places. His first open-air sermon was preached on February 17, 1739, on a knoll in Bristol before two hundred miners. After that, the numbers in his outdoor audiences increased.

Whitefield possessed the gifts which were needed for open-air preaching. Without doubt, he may be called one of the truly great preachers of Christendom, certainly in delivery of his sermons if not from the point of view of content. David Garrick, a popular English actor of the eighteenth century, said that Whitefield could melt an audience simply by pronouncing the word, "Mesopotamia." He said that he would cheerfully give a hundred guineas for the ability to say "O" as Whitefield said it.[2]

Once while Whitefield was preaching in Philadelphia, Benja-

[2] Stuart C. Henry, *George Whitefield: Wayfaring Witness* (Nashville: Abingdon Press, 1957), p. 61.

min Franklin tested the distance his voice would carry. He concluded that Whitefield could be heard by an outdoor audience of thirty thousand.[3] But Franklin's relations with Whitefield were not always cold and scientific. Knowing something of the power Whitefield could exert upon an audience, Franklin vowed that when the offering was taken he would not give a penny. However, when the sermon was over, Poor Richard had emptied his pockets into the collection plate. Franklin mentioned the conversions which followed the meeting; for as he went about over the city he heard "psalms ringing out from house after house." A warm friendship developed between the two. When Franklin's experiments in electricity were being widely discussed, Whitefield wrote to him: "I find that you grow more and more famous in the learned world. As you have made a pretty considerable progress in the mysteries of electricity, I would now humbly recommend to your diligent unprejudiced pursuit and study the mystery of the new birth." [4]

Whitefield's labors live on through the help that he gave to the educational institutions then struggling for existence in America. When the library at Harvard College was destroyed by fire, he helped to raise the funds needed to rebuild it. He gave encouragement to the establishment of Dartmouth College by the Earl of Dartmouth, Secretary of Colonial Affairs, an institution projected at first as a missionary enterprise for Indians. He had many associations with Gilbert Tennant, the founder of the institutions culminating in Princeton University. In 1757, Princeton College conferred upon him an honorary degree. He wanted a college to be established in Georgia at Bethesda and requested a grant of two thousand acres for it. This failed, partly

[3] Francis Tees, *The Beginnings of Methodism in America* (Nashville: Parthenon Press, 1940), p. 63.
[4] Henry, *op. cit.*, p. 87.

because Whitefield would not agree for it to be a college of the Church of England.[5] The University of Pennsylvania grew out of his labors and a statue standing on the grounds attests to his connection with its beginnings.

Whitefield made seven visits to colonial America. All the churches of that day owe much to his powerful ministrations. Everywhere he went he found that a more "effectual door opened than ever before for preaching the gospel."

Lacking the organizational gifts of Wesley, however, Whitefield did not form his converts into classes. Joseph Pilmoor, one of the first two Methodist preachers sent by Wesley, who personally visited all parts of the country, noted that there were many thousands of persons who had been "deeply affected and savingly wrought under Whitefield's ministry." Reforms and civilizing influences followed his labors. His interest in the founding of schools and orphanages connects his name with the founding of the University of Pennsylvania and Dartmouth College. Lord Dartmouth was a frequent attendant at the services that he conducted at Bath, England.

Whitefield's work has not been closely associated with the development of early Methodism because of the doctrinal difference between him and Wesley. Whitefield, a Calvinist, held that God intended to give saving grace through Christ only to a limited number and that the rest of mankind, because of the fall of Adam, would be left by God to continue in sin and would ultimately be condemned to eternal death.

Wesley, an Arminian, held to the doctrine of free grace, a system which took its name from the Dutch theologian, Jacobus Arminius. John and Charles Wesley preached that Christ's atonement was unlimited and open to all who believed in him. In contrast to the Calvinists, they put stress upon personal freedom.

[5] *Ibid.,* p. 93.

They held that redeeming grace could be resisted by the impenitent sinner. They also preached that a sinner once regenerated might backslide and die in his sins. "Backsliding" is a word which belongs in the Methodist vocabulary.

The lines of American Methodism go back to three European countries—England, Germany, and Ireland. However, the direct line of descent for the first Methodist work goes back to Ireland. The first two Methodist societies in Maryland and New York were founded by persons who had been converted in Ireland under John Wesley. Wesley made forty-two visits to that country. On one of his visits there he found a community of Protestants who had been driven from their homes in Germany by Louis XIV of France in one of his efforts to place the boundary of France at the Rhine. Without religious influence, they had become a thoroughly demoralized people, drunkenness, profanity, Sabbath breaking, and religious illiteracy prevailing among them. Under Methodist preaching, these German Protestants were changed into serious-thinking, devout people. Among them was Philip Embury, who organized the first class in New York. In the records about his conversion in Ireland, he left this item: "On Christmas day . . . in the year of 1752, the Lord shone into my soul by a glimpse of his redeeming love, being an earnest of my redemption in Christ Jesus, to whom be glory for ever and ever. Amen." [6]

Embury, with a party of Irish-Germans, including Barbara Heck, Embury's cousin, arrived in New York in 1760. These immigrants, soon enamored of the material concerns of the New World, drifted away from their former Methodist moorings. Embury, backslidden along with the rest, had quit exhorting and had ceased to have any concern for the moral needs of

[6] Abel Stevens, *History of the Methodist Episcopal Church* (New York: Carlton & Porter, 1864), I, 54.

his community. On a visit that she made to one of the homes, Barbara Heck found a group playing cards and gambling. She seized the cards, threw them into the fire, and called upon the people to give up their evil ways. While still stirred by her concerns, she rushed to the home of Philip Embury and cried: "Brother Embury, you must preach to us or we shall all go to hell, and God will require our blood at your hands!" [7] When Embury excused his inactivity by saying he had neither a house nor a congregation, she retorted, "Preach in your own house and to your own company first." Embury, himself aroused, began to hold services. Soon the Methodist congregation was too large for the Embury house.

When the first Methodist society of poor immigrants in New York outgrew the Embury house, a rigging loft eighteen by sixty feet was rented. This, too, soon was not large enough to care for the people who wanted to attend the meetings. Plans were laid for a new church. In 1768 the first house of worship was erected. It was a stone chapel, forty-two by sixty feet. In New York, where there was an established tax-supported church, the state law did not permit any other faith to build a church. Consequently, to avoid legal complications it was necessary to build the church in the form of a dwelling house, including a fireplace and chimney. The new meetinghouse became the first of the many "Wesley Chapels" in America.

The adventure, however, would not have been possible at this time if it had not been for a man of some financial means and local prestige. He was Captain Thomas Webb of the king's service, one of the most colorful figures in early Methodism. After being converted, Webb joined the Methodists in England and was licensed to preach by Wesley. When he heard of the

[7] Halford E. Luccock, Paul Hutchinson, and Robert W. Goodloe, *The Story of Methodism* (rev. ed.; Nashville: Abingdon Press), pp. 145, 146.

41

organizing of this Methodist Society in New York, he left his home in Albany to visit it and offer his encouragement.

Soon Webb's presence about New York, and especially his preaching, became widely noticed. He made a striking appearance; for he wore his full uniform and laid his sword across the pulpit. At the siege of Louisburg he lost an eye, and pictures of him always show his wearing a green patch over the socket. A fervent and eloquent man, he drew large crowds to hear him. John Adams, who once heard him preach, said he was "one of the most eloquent men I ever heard; he reaches the imagination and touches the passions." [8]

Captain Webb remained in America until the outbreak of the war, when he returned to England. He preached in many parts of the country. He is credited with organizing Methodist Societies around New York, New Jersey, and Philadelphia. At Philadelphia, he helped the small society to acquire a church from a German Reformed congregation. This building is still standing and is known as St. George Methodist Church. It has been in continuous use by Methodists longer than any other church in the United States.

Webb persistently appealed to Wesley for preachers for the colonies. Wesley, however, thought he was overly optimistic about the future of the new country. Wesley could not imagine that New York, then with a population of only twenty thousand, would ever become a rival of Bristol in importance. Charles Wesley dismissed Webb as "an inexperienced, honest, zealous, loving enthusiast." The Methodist historian William Warren Sweet thinks that Webb deserves more credit than any other person for firmly planting the Methodist movement on American soil.

The founder of Methodist work in Maryland, Robert Straw-

---

[8] *Ibid.,* p. 147.

bridge, migrated from Leitrim, Ireland. He, too, had been converted in Ireland under the ministry of John Wesley. There, in spite of Catholic opposition, he became a faithful, devout, and zealous local preacher under Wesley's influence. The fires kindled in his soul did not go out in the new country. Upon his arrival, he immediately began preaching, first in his own house and later in a log church that he built. This log meetinghouse was to be the prototype of hundreds of humble Methodist chapels built by pioneers in the New World. This, some hold, was the first Methodist meetinghouse erected in America.

Strawbridge was the first preacher to serve as a full-time Methodist itinerant in America. His preaching trips took him to eastern Maryland, Delaware, Pennsylvania, and northern Virginia. Often while he was away his neighbors cultivated his crops. Many of his converts migrated across the Alleghenies, thus carrying the coals to kindle revival fires in the new West. Some of the first itinerants, including William Watters, Thomas Bond, and Freeborn Garrettson, were called to the ministry under Strawbridge's labors.

Strawbridge was impatient with the slowness of Methodist leaders to set up an independent church. He, himself, in violation of Wesley's rule, administered the sacraments. His independent attitude made it difficult for him to accept the disciplines which Asbury expected of his preachers.

American Methodism before 1769 had advanced under lay preachers and without any direct connection with Wesley. Previously, there had been no evidence that Wesley included America in his plans. The prosperity of the new societies had from the first encouraged the leaders to believe that a great and effectual door was open to Methodism in the new country. Thomas Taylor of New York, in a letter to Wesley, asked him "for the good of thousands" to send an able and experienced preacher, a "man of wisdom, of sound faith, and a good disciplinarian: one whose heart and soul are in the work." If this kind of leadership could be given, he said, "a flame will be soon kindled as would never stop until it reached the great South Sea." [9] If necessary, these first American Methodists told Wesley, they were willing to sell their own "coats and shirts" to provide money for passage of the preacher.

At the Methodist conference in 1769, Wesley announced that he had received pressing calls from "our brethren in New York to come over and help them." He called for volunteers. Two preachers, Richard Boardman and Joseph Pilmoor, responded. As a token of "brotherly love" the conference took up a collection to pay for the transportation of the two missionaries. Because of the poverty of early Methodists the sacrifices made to plant the work in America were equivalent to the giving of "coats and shirts." [10]

Pilmoor reached America in his thirtieth year. After he had been converted under Wesley at sixteen, he spent four years in Kingswood School studying English literature, Latin, Hebrew, and Greek. Boardman was born in Ireland and had traveled circuits in that country.

The departure of these emissaries of Methodism to take charge of the work in the New World was of such great importance to Wesley and his colleagues that they carefully prepared the men for it. George Whitefield gave them extended counsel about the new country. Pilmoor noted then that the "difference in theological views between Wesley and Whitefield made no difference in love and affection." Charles Wesley also had a conference with them "where he spoke freely and kindly to us

[9] Tees, op. cit., p. 100.
[10] Ibid., p. 104.

about our sea voyage and the important business in which we had engaged."

The lack of communication made it impossible for American Methodists to know when to expect the newly appointed workers. Their ship landed six miles below Philadelphia. They walked that distance to the city. A man who had been in the society in Ireland with Boardman recognized him and Pilmoor and put them in communication with Captain Webb and other Philadelphia Methodists.

The two preachers immediately assumed responsibility for Methodist work. Boardman went to New York while Pilmoor took over at Philadelphia. In accordance with the Methodist itinerary, they exchanged places every three months.

Another Irish Methodist preacher, Robert Williams, about whom more will be said in Chapter VII, heard of the call from America. He resolved to be the first itinerant to arrive. Wesley did not approve of his going, but when he had agreed to serve under Boardman and Pilmoor, Wesley gave his consent. After selling his horse to pay his debts, Williams did not have money for passage but set out for the port carrying his saddlebags on his arm. An Irish friend met him there and paid his passage.

Williams pioneered in Virginia and North Carolina. He was the spiritual father of Jesse Lee, apostle to New England and one of the greatest of the first American preachers.

Eight missionaries in all were sent by Wesley to America. In 1773 when the first Methodist conference was held in America, 10 preachers and 1,160 members were reported. From that year Methodists have tabulated faithfully each year the number of members, lay and clerical. (Is it any wonder Methodists are conscious of statistics?) In answer to the question, "How are the preachers stationed?" six appointments were made: New York, Philadelphia, New Jersey, Baltimore, Norfolk, Petersburg.

CHAPTER IV

A Church Is Born

THE YEARS 1773 AND 1784 WERE YEARS OF DECISION FOR the Methodist Societies in America. During this period the Societies composed a circuit on the list of appointments of English Methodism. They were under the direct control of John Wesley. He wanted Methodists to be one people and rebuffed any talk of independence. The Revolutionary War made changes inevitable, however. Most of the clergy of the Church of England left America during the war. Likewise, all the Methodist preachers sent over by Wesley except Asbury went home. Asbury cast his lot with the young Societies: "It would be an eternal dishonor to the Methodists that we should all leave the three thousand souls who desire to commit themselves to our care; neither is it the part of the Good Shepherd to leave his flock in time of danger. Therefore I am determined, by the grace of God, not to leave them, let the consequence be what it may." [1]

Francis Asbury had volunteered to go to the colonies at the conference in Bristol in 1771, after hearing John Wesley say that more preachers were needed in America. He was then twenty-six years old and had traveled under Wesley for six years. Asbury had a Methodist experience. He wrote that, while praying in his father's barn, "the Lord pardoned my sins and justified my soul." [2] He was licensed to preach at seventeen and

[1] E. S. Tipple, *Francis Asbury: The Prophet of the Long Road* (Cincinnati: The Methodist Book Concern, 1916), p. 126.
[2] *Journal and Letters*, I, 721.

at twenty-one gave up his work in a blacksmith's shop to enter the Methodist ministry. Five years later, in 1771, he landed in Philadelphia. He served the Methodist cause in North America for forty-five years without returning to his native country. His name furnishes the peg on which much of the story of the organization of The Methodist Church in the United States is hung.

Because of their connection with John Wesley, American Methodists were regarded by the supporters of the Revolution as Tories or friends of King George. Before the war began John Wesley had opposed the use of force against the Americans and had asked Lord North to consider sympathetically the demands of the colonists for their legal rights. After war was declared, however, Wesley defended England's course and issued a "Calm Address to the American Colonists" censuring their resistance to the British government and defending the tax placed upon the colonies. This publication had wide use in England; forty thousand copies were distributed at the doors of all churches in London. It caused the loyalty of American Methodists to be suspect. In some places the opposition was bitter and violent.

Asbury expressed regret that Wesley had dipped into the politics of America. Since he knew Wesley's temperament, Asbury apologetically remarked that "had he been a subject of America he would have been a zealous advocate of the American cause." As the recognized leader of colonial Methodists, Asbury held the Societies together during the war years. He had lived here long enough to understand the attitude of American leaders toward self-government, though he may not have accepted it as his own. He sensed that Methodism in America would have to dissociate itself from the mother country and determine its own destiny. In time Methodism would fully identify itself with the equalitarian aims of the new country.

Under Asbury, Methodist circuit riders would be important influences in establishing freedom for all.

Generally speaking, Methodists of that day were patriots at heart. Many served in the colonial army, though some refused, out of conscience, to bear arms or take the test oath. Jesse Lee, while unwilling to carry a gun, did consent to drive a baggage wagon. Richard Allen, founder of the African Methodist Church, was also a noncombatant in the Revolutionary War and hauled salt for the Continental Army.[3]

From the very first, Methodism in America was handicapped in its work by not having the rights belonging to a church. The preachers could not baptize their converts nor administer the Lord's Supper to them. For the sacraments American Methodists had to look to the clergy of the established church, a group often out of sympathy with their efforts. This was complicated further when war reduced the number of Anglican clergymen in America. Methodist preachers grew restive at Wesley's refusal to allow them to administer the sacraments. Asbury, who had been compelled because of anti-Methodist feelings to give up traveling and go into seclusion, risked arrest to attend a conference of Methodist preachers in Virginia who threatened to break Wesley's rule. Asbury urged patience until he could lay the matter before Wesley.

Fortunately for the Methodist movement, Wesley could rise above his prejudices. His mind was never shut completely. Time and time again the high churchman departed from tradition to meet the practical problems of the Methodist movement. Now he knew that the new relationship of America to his country called for adjustments.

At this point, the question was, Does the Church of England

[3] *The Life Experience and Gospel Labors of the Rt. Rev. Richard Allen* (Nashville: Abingdon Press, 1960), p. 9.

have the exclusive right to set aside through ordination those who would be its ministers? Wesley had not raised it before, because, as some believed, he hoped the bishops of his church would eventually concede and ordain Methodist associates.

When Wesley was convinced that the bishops would not give holy orders to his preachers, he met the "logic of events" and acted in a way that was in direct opposition to all the antecedents of his life. Since the breach between him and his church could not be healed, he moved to make the Societies in America into a church. He said: "My scruples are at an end; and I conceive myself at full liberty, as I violate no order, and invade no man's rights, by appointing and sending labourers into the harvest." [4] What happened from this point on forms an important chapter in church history.

Scholars usually attribute Wesley's bold departure from Church-of-England tenets on ordination to a book written by Lord Peter King on the primitive church. In the primitive church there were two orders of the clergy, deacons and elders, and the episcopacy was not an order but an office. This meant that presbyters could set aside one of their number as a bishop. In line with this plan Wesley prescribed for America an episcopal form of church polity, with superintendents, deacons, and elders. This does not mean that he regarded it as a form sanctioned in the Scriptures. He held this view once, but concluded later that neither Christ nor his apostles gave any directive for a form of church government and that the plea of divine right for diocesan episcopacy was never heard of in the primitive church. When pressed, Wesley defended his position by saying, "I firmly believe, I am a scriptural *episkopas,* as much as any other man in England or in Europe. For the uninterrupted succession [the Anglican doctrine which declares that

⁴ Tyerman, *op. cit.,* III, 435.

the church's ministry is derived from the Apostles by a continuing mystic transmission of spiritual authority through the episcopacy] I know to be a fable." [5]

Acting in line with these conclusions, Wesley appointed Thomas Coke, a presbyter of the Church of England, to be a superintendent and designated him to take charge of Methodist Societies in America. He also ordained Richard Whatcoat and Thomas Vasey as deacons and elders. These two, with Coke, sailed for America on September 18, 1784, carrying a letter from Wesley which granted American Methodists the right to organize an independent episcopal church. Wesley also authorized Coke to name Asbury a general superintendent. Concerning this decision, Wesley wrote: "I took a step which I had long weighed and appointed three of our brethren to go and serve the desolate sheep in America which I verily believe will be much to the glory of God." The letter which Coke carried from Wesley recites not only his conclusions but the thought processes which led up to them.[6]

Thomas Coke, an Anglican clergyman, was educated at Jesus College, Oxford. After graduation, while "an unregenerated man," as he said, he became the minister of South Petherton parish. Here a friend loaned him the sermons of Wesley; these aroused in him a desire to know about religious faith as taught by the Methodists. Thomas Maxfield, the first local preacher under Wesley who had obtained ordination and was pastor of an independent congregation at Petherton, and a Methodist class leader who was a laborer on a rich man's estate, helped Coke to become acquainted with the evangelical way of salvation. This new experience brought fervor and earnestness not previously known to Coke's preaching. Through Coke many

[5] *Works*, XIII, 253.
[6] Stevens, *op. cit.*, II, 182-83.

were awakened. Soon opposition developed, however, and Coke was dismissed from the church. In 1778 he became actively identified with the Methodists. He traveled extensively under Wesley's direction. Wesley recognized his leadership and administrative gifts and committed to him many responsibilities, among them presiding at the first session of the Irish conference in 1782. When Wesley saw that the organization of American Methodists was an imperative, he chose Coke to carry out the plan, and on September 1, 1784, ordained him as superintendent of the Methodist Societies in America.

Coke and his associates, Whatcoat and Vasey, landed in New York on November 3, 1784. From an entry in Coke's journal we may infer that their coming was not entirely unexpected. Reports of the discussions between Wesley and others on the organization of a church had reached America and their appearance had been expected. This sense of expectancy likely rose from the promise Asbury had made to the American preachers at the Fluvanna Conference in Virginia that he would work with Wesley on a plan to permit them to administer the holy sacraments. John Dickins, then preacher in charge in New York, and one who had been demanding ministerial rights, welcomed Coke. When Wesley's plan was explained, he emphatically approved it and urged Coke to announce it. Wesley had spoken, and as far as Dickins was concerned that had settled the matter. Coke, however, decided not to disclose it until he had consulted with Asbury.

Coke met Asbury at Barratt's Chapel in Delaware on Sunday, November 14, 1784. There he outlined Wesley's directive for organizing the Methodists of America into a church and making him one of the general superintendents. Asbury agreed to the plan with one exception, namely, that he would not become a general superintendent by an appointment made by Wesley. He would accept only if elected by the preachers.

Wesley had not intended to grant this power to American preachers. Born and bred a Tory, he did not have a high estimate of democratic procedures. He once admitted that he was a dictator, a fact which any student of Methodist history accepts. Under Wesley, English Methodism was a benevolent dictatorship—all authority was vested in him. Asbury, after living thirteen years in America, was aware of the democratic sentiment prevailing in the new republic. He knew that American Methodists would insist upon being allowed to share in the decisions concerning their work.

The departure from Wesley's instructions was destined to have far-reaching effects upon the development of Methodism in America. It meant that the Methodist Conference in America was not to be just a discussion group but a legislative body. In the English conferences, while free discussion was permitted, final decisions were made by Wesley. Asbury's decision meant the uniting of democratic procedures to the episcopal form of church government.

Coke and Asbury agreed that Wesley's proposal should be placed before the preachers. Freeborn Garrettson was sent "like an arrow" to call together all the Methodist preachers in the United States. In six weeks he rode twelve hundred miles. (Some of the preachers did not get word; among them was Jesse Lee, who charged Garrettson with doing too much preaching on the way.)

On December 24, 1784, sixty of the eighty-three Methodist preachers assembled at Lovely Lane Chapel, Baltimore, Maryland, for the purpose of organizing the Methodists of North America into a church.

The American founders of the church were young and inexperienced. Most of them were under thirty years of age, the average age being twenty-six. Of the eighty-three preachers eligible for membership in the conference, only eleven were married, and only sixteen had served as many as five years in the itineracy.

Lovely Lane Chapel was a plain structure, the only kind Methodists of that day could afford. Its members, Coke said, were so "kind as to put up a large stove and to back several of the seats."

Asbury said: "We spent the whole week in conference, debating freely, and determining all things by a majority of votes. The Doctor [Coke] preached every day at noon, and some one of the other preachers morning and evening. We were in great haste, and did much business in a little time." [7]

In line with Wesley's letter of directions and Asbury's amendments, the conference voted to form the Methodists of America into an episcopal church. John Dickins proposed the name, "Methodist Episcopal Church." Asbury and Coke were unanimously elected general superintendents. Asbury, who up to this time was just a local preacher, was ordained a deacon one day and an elder on the next. On the third day he was consecrated general superintendent.

While he was a missionary in Georgia, Wesley had witnessed a Moravian ordination service. Commenting on it, he wrote: "The great simplicity, as well as the solemnity . . . made me forget the seventeen hundred years between, and imagine myself in one of those assemblies where form and state were not, but Paul the tent-maker, or Peter the fisherman presided, yet with the demonstration of the Spirit and of power." [8] Had he looked in on the ordination of Asbury and others at Lovely Lane in

[7] *Journal and Letters*, I, 476.
[8] *Journal*, I, 170.

1784, he would have seen enacted on American soil a scene reminiscent of the primitive church.

Wesley's methodical planning for the church is seen in the instruments he sent. One was the twenty-four articles of religion adapted from the Thirty-Nine Articles of the Anglican Church. Wesley's personal views of the church and the progress of his thinking may be discovered by noting his abridgement of the Thirty-Nine Articles. The conference added on its own one which said that "the states should not be subject to any foreign jurisdiction." Wesley also sent a Sunday worship service which he prepared, but it was more formal than was suited to early American Methodists. Among the rules adopted was the one prohibiting the preachers from drinking intoxicating liquors except for medicinal purposes.

The salary fixed for a preacher was sixty-four dollars annually; if married he received the same amount for his wife and sixteen dollars for each child under six years of age. Plans for a "preachers' fund" and for the relief of superannuated preachers and widows were adopted.

The purposeful plan of evangelism was shown in the instructions the conference gave to its preachers:

You have nothing to do but to save souls. Go always not only to those that want but to those that want you most. Observe. It is not your business to preach so many times and to take care of this or that society, but to bring as many sinners as you possibly can to repentance, and with all your power to build them up in that holiness, without which they cannot see the Lord!

For carrying out the work of encouraging the people in holiness, the conference included these rules in the first *Discipline:*

Go into every house and teach everyone therein, young and old, to be Christian inwardly and outwardly. Make every particular plain to their understanding; fix it in their memory; write it on their heart. In order to do this there must be line upon line, precept upon precept. What patience, what love, what knowledge is requisite for this.

Where there are ten children, meet them at least an hour every week.

Will you diligently instruct the children in every place?

Talk with them every time you see any of them at home.

Diligently instruct and vehemently exhort the parents at their own houses.

Preach expressly on education. "But I have no gift for this." Gift or no gift, you are to do it, else you are not called to be a Methodist preacher. Do it as you can until you can do it as you would. Pray earnestly for the gift and use the means for it.

Along with the evangelistic note, the Christmas Conference put into the life of the new church the special concerns to be identified with its future. The Methodist Episcopal Church was to be a missionary church. From Lovely Lane the first Methodist missionaries went out. Education was to be associated with its evangelistic efforts. Here Methodists took the first steps to build institutions of higher learning. Methodism's capacity for indignation toward evils detrimental to the welfare of persons was reflected here. The resolution adopted by that conference against slavery shows how deeply these young preachers felt about the major social wrong of their day. In spite of all the vast growth of this denomination, it is difficult to isolate any special concern regarded as important today that did not exist in some form at the Lovely Lane conference.

The Methodist Episcopal Church at its inception became an independent, self-contained church. While the preachers revered Wesley and at the Christmas Conference acknowledged themselves to be "his sons in the gospel, ready in matters belonging to church government to obey his commands," they reserved the right to pass on his recommendations. When Wesley directed that Richard Whatcoat and Freeborn Garrettson be made superintendents, they refused to elect them.

In 1787 the title of general superintendent gave way to "bishop." This historic name fitted into the episcopal form of government adopted. Wesley did not concur with the change. He wrote to Asbury: "How can you, how dare you suffer yourself to be called Bishop? I shudder, I start, at the very thought! Men may call me a knave or a fool, a rascal, a scoundrel, and I am content: but they shall never by my consent call me Bishop! For my sake, for God's sake, for Christ's sake put a full end to this!" [9]

The Christmas Conference did not make provision for any future meeting such as we have come to know in the General Conference. Regional conferences were held annually, but they did not meet the need. A council composed of the bishops and presiding elders was created to consider matters involving the needs of the church. This council was without authority to make its actions final until they had been approved by the conference.

The council did not prove practical, and after two sessions, it was abandoned. In 1792 another church-wide meeting of the preachers was called with 266 present. Following this one, there were quadrennial meetings to which all preachers were asked to come. Experiences pointed the way for an effective organization. In 1808 a constitution was adopted. The General Conference was made the supreme legislative body of the church. Ministerial delegates after this date were elected by the annual conferences on a quota basis according to membership. The plan of representation by clerical delegates continued

[9] William W. Sweet, *Methodism in American History* (Nashville: Abingdon Press, 1953), p. 116.

until provision was made almost one hundred years later to admit laymen.

The annual conferences grew in importance as the church grew. Between 1785 and the General Conference of 1792 they passed on legislation proposed by the general superintendents. Until the plan for the General Conference was fixed, the annual conferences were regarded as local or sectional meetings of the one undivided ministry and were held in different sections for the convenience of the ministers. There were three such annual meetings in 1787. As the church grew the number of annual conferences increased and their responsibilities centered about the regions they served.

The annual conference is considered the basic unit of The Methodist Church. At first its proceedings consisted of a series of questions and answers. The last question, "Where are the preachers stationed for this year?" prompted the reading of the list of appointments prepared for the next conference year. The preachers at the outset, and until comparatively recent years, had no knowledge of their assignments until they were announced by the bishops. Thus, the reading of the list of appointments was a dramatic moment—and often one of disappointment. In the early days, as Abel Stevens said, "The reading of the list was like the announcement of an order of battle. It was heard by the militant itinerants with ejaculations of prayer, with sobs, and shouts." [10]

When it was organized the new church was the weakest among the denominations then at work in the United States. It had but one preacher who could be called "liberally educated." The task it laid out looked like an impossible one. But the statistics compiled annually by the conferences told of the

[10] *Op. cit.*, II, 222.

church's phenomenal growth against seemingly impossible obstacles.

The explanation behind this growth is found in the man chosen as the leader, Francis Asbury, a great spiritual strategist. He had been in this country but a few weeks when he observed that there was insufficient circulation among the preachers. They did not want to leave the cities and go into the country where the people were to preach. "My brethren," he wrote in his journal less than one month after he arrived, "seem unwilling to leave the cities, but I think I shall show them the way." [11] Seeing that preachers were sent to the people became the ruling passion of his life.

Asbury took up his episcopal duties two days after the Christmas Conference adjourned and rode fifty miles through "frost and snow" to Fairfax, Virginia. In the forty-five years he labored in this country, Asbury traveled 270,000 miles, an average of about 6,000 miles each year, through pathless forests and untraveled wilderness, among the swamps and heat of the South and the snows of New England. He ordained 4,000 preachers and presided over 224 conferences. Wherever he went he preached—16,425 sermons, or an average of one for each day for forty-five years. He never had an episcopal residence, but established his headquarters in the saddle. His area was the whole United States. Once when he was asked where he was from, he replied, "From Boston, New York, Philadelphia, Baltimore, or almost any place you please." [12]

Asbury's plan of sending preachers to the people caused Methodism to expand with the republic. He sent James Haw in 1786 to the uncivilized wilderness beyond the Appalachian

[11] *Journal and Letters*, I, 10.
[12] Paul N. Garber, *Romance of American Methodism* (Greensboro, N. C.: The Piedmont Press, 1931), p. 48. Used by permission.

Mountains. The next year Haw returned to the conference in Baltimore and called for preachers to serve with him in the new country. In 1787 two ministers were assigned to a circuit consisting of all of Kentucky and middle Tennessee. Asbury never asked his preachers to go anywhere he was not willing to follow. In 1790 he set out to go to visit the new country Haw had opened up for the church. It was a hazardous undertaking. An armed company of fifteen men met the bishop at Cumberland Gap, Virginia, to escort him to Lexington, Kentucky, the place set for the conference. Apparently Asbury carried a rifle on the trip; for a powder horn with his name and the date, May, 1790, is in existence.

Asbury was the first Protestant bishop to cross the Alleghenies. His journal gives an account of it:

I was strangely outdone for want of sleep, having been greatly deprived of it in my journey through the wilderness; which is like being at sea, in some respects, and in others worse. Our way is over mountains, steep hills, deep rivers, and muddy creeks; the thick growth of reeds for miles together; and no inhabitants but wild beasts and savage men. Sometimes, before I am aware, my ideas would be leading me to be looking out ahead for a fence; and I would, without reflection, try to recollect the houses we should have lodged at in the wilderness. I slept about an hour the first night, and about two the last; we ate no regular meal; our bread grew short, and I was much spent.[13]

While Asbury was continually on the go, he was never well. His ailments were legion and his journal is replete with references to them, together with the remedies he applied. Once he took the itch. Commenting on it, he wrote, "Considering the filthy houses and filthy beds I have met with, it is a perhaps strange thing that I have not caught it 20 times. I do not see that there is any security against it but by sleeping in a brimstone shirt."

[13] *Journal and Letters,* I, 636.

Asbury, like the other Methodist preachers, did not have a formal education. But doubtless inspired by Wesley, he became a lover of learning and a persistent student. One who carefully examined Asbury's journal found his range of reading covered practically the whole field of literature and science of that day. He read books of history, biography, theology, and sermonic literature. But with all this wide reading he did not neglect his Bible. He carried with him on his travels a Hebrew Bible. He had been taught the elements of Hebrew grammar by John Wesley at Bristol. He noted once that he had read the Bible through in four months. This he did by rising at four or five o'clock—long enough each morning to read before breakfast.[14] His conversations with his preachers show that he did not live on the surface intellectually. The monument erected to him in the nation's capital appropriately portrays him on horseback with an open book in his hand.

In spite of his demand for democratic procedures in the organization of the church, Asbury did not practice democracy in his administration. He kept control of the appointments of preachers. His personal knowledge of the country and its needs equipped him to do this. In retrospect we may say that this may be seen as a vital element in the success of early Methodism. Asbury's administration was tempered with a deep love for the preachers and their work. In one conference where the preachers were too poor to buy decent clothes, he acted to help them. He wrote, "I parted with my watch, my coat, and my shirt." Elmer T. Clark in his introduction to *The Journal and Letters of Francis Asbury* paid this tribute to him: "He loved his preachers next to God. He accepted the same small salary, endured the same hardships, lived the same life, and traveled more than any of them. He asked nothing of them that he did

---

[14] Tipple, *op. cit.*, p. 103.

not impose upon himself; and they knew that if he sent them on hard rounds, he had already made harder rounds and would make more." [15]

Asbury's life was intimately interwoven with the new nation's. He knew the United States as few of his contemporaries did. His journal furnishes insights for the study of the history of the nation in its beginning years. This fact was recognized when the National Historical Publications Commission of the United States Government included Asbury among the sixty-six great Americans whose works the body recommended for proper editing and publication, along with Washington, Jefferson, Adams, Lincoln, and other immortals of the land.[16]

[15] Introduction, I, xiv.
[16] *Ibid.*, I, xv.

CHAPTER V

The Circuit Rider

SOMEONE HAS SAID THAT AMERICAN CHRISTIANITY'S FIRST order of business after winning the battle against England was to wrest the new nation from the control of the devil. The moral and religious conditions of that period make this a statement of fact, not a humorous pun. War and religion do not mix. The patriots were dedicated primarily to the cause of independence. Religious concern was secondary, if considered at all. Apart from the war, certain other attitudes held toward Christianity were injurious to its development. One was a form of religion called deism. In this religion the Christian faith faced in the closing years of the eighteenth century one of its most dangerous threats.

In America, as in England, deism flourished among the intellectuals. Many of the founding fathers and persons holding high positions of public trust openly avowed their disbelief in the word of God. Nathan Bangs says that the minds of many people were corrupted by the deistic writings of Thomas Paine "whose effusions against the Bible were received with greater avidity by Americans on account of the eminent services he had rendered to his country during the war of the revolution." [1]

Dean Willard L. Sperry of Harvard mentions the influence of this movement upon the framers of our Constitution. He says:

[1] *History of the Methodist Episcopal Church* (New York: T. Mason and G. Lane, 1839, out of print), II, 21.

It is impossible . . . to resist the conclusion that in its date the framing of the Constitution of the United States coincided with the late eighteenth-century cult of rationalism, and that the prevalence of enlightened deistic ideas among educated classes was in part responsible for the studied silences of the document as to the existence of God, and its unwillingness to commit itself, even in the most general terms, to any Christian ideas.[2]

The ties formed between America and France during the Revolution helped spread here the spirit of religious skepticism that was rampant abroad. As in modern Russia, the leaders of the French Revolution had repudiated the church and made plans for a new social order in which Christianity would be discarded as outmoded and obsolete. This same contempt for religion influenced American sympathizers with the French Revolution. Infidelity and religious indifference were not limited to the Atlantic seaboard but reached into the hunting camps and log cabins of the new West.

A breakdown of morals inevitably follows lapses in religious beliefs. William W. Sweet, the distinguished church historian, said: "In the period of the Revolution, and in the years immediately following, religious and moral conditions of the country as a whole reached the lowest ebb tide in the entire history of the American people." [3]

Mass migrations also diminished concern for the Christian faith. When people are uprooted from established communities and transplanted to new environments, they do not always carry their moral and religious traditions. In the history of the settling of the American frontier the baser passions were given full rein. Indian warfare, land speculation, rough sports, fighting,

---

[2] *Religion in America* (New York: The Macmillan Company, 1946), p. 58.
[3] *Revivalism in America* (New York: Charles Scribner's Sons, 1944, out of print), p. 117.

drinking, and gambling contributed to the corruption and loose living in the West. Good people were shocked at the vice encountered everywhere in the new country.

On the frontier Asbury often found many persons he had known in the Eastern states who were in a backslidden condition. Good land he found, rarely makes people any better. He discovered, too, that it did not arouse concern for religion. Not more than 4 per cent of the first settlers beyond the mountains, a pioneer Presbyterian missionary found, were church members, and, as he said, the people were ignorant of religion.

This may also be called a period of ineffectiveness for the churches themselves. The Anglican Church's loyalty to England made it suspect. Its ministers, the patriots knew, did not sympathize with the Revolution.

In appraising the moral and religious life of the republic, we must realize that ecclesiastical as well as political independence from the mother country was expected. The founding fathers, furthermore, required full separation between the church and the state. At the time of the Revolution nine of the thirteen colonies had established churches supported by taxes. Disestablishment of the state churches, particularly the Anglican ones, was effected immediately. The future of the church at this point in our history depended upon its ability to prove that Christianity and equalitarian democracy could live together.

The Methodist Church was destined to play an important role in the life of the new republic. Its organization in 1784 made it the first indigenous episcopal church in America (the Protestant Episcopal Church came in 1789). The break with English Methodism was clear cut. The American Methodists promptly identified their destinies with the new republic, as shown in the twenty-five articles of religion adopted at the Christmas Conference. In 1789 the conference meeting in New

York delegated its bishops, Asbury and Coke, to declare formally the allegiance of the Methodist Church to the republic.

The preachers knew the basic purposes of the new republic and readily assumed responsibility for interpreting them. This they did in the remote parts of the country far beyond the established centers of civilization. Once when Jacob Young was working with Lorenzo Dow in a camp meeting in the remote Mississippi country near Natchez, some persons present created a disturbance. Dow rebuked them and then gave the assembly a discourse on the civil gains made in America through the Revolution. In it he repeated from memory the whole Constitution and then showed how it served as the center of gravity, keeping every state in its place. The preachers, without question, were most formidable influences in establishing understanding of both citizenship and morality in the new republic.

Asbury accepted the challenge presented by eighteenth-century America. He knew the country and was aware of the responsibilities entailed. His first task was to recruit and train ministers. Here again the "train of providences" mentioned by Wesley in his letter explaining his decision to form a separate church in the United States was apparent. The divine hand may be seen in the preachers who were raised up to meet the peculiar needs of the church in the new nation. Rugged young men who were able to defend themselves against Indians, "bad men," and wild animals on the frontier were chosen. Very few, if any, of the first preachers could be called experienced. They were so young that they formed a veritable youth crusade. Henry Bascom was only seventeen when he received his first appointment of twenty-seven preaching places. Joshua Soule joined the New England Conference at eighteen. By the time he was twenty-three he had been appointed presiding elder of a Maine district.

In 1790 at the first conference held west of the Alleghenies, four of the six preachers who received appointments were under twenty-five. Bishop Galloway once said that thousands of Methodist preachers were riding circuits before they were old enough to vote or needed to use a razor. Many, like Benjamin Ogden, one of the first itinerants to cross the mountains into the Western wilderness, and Francis McCormick, the first Methodist preacher in Ohio, were veterans of the Revolutionary War. "Veteran" meant in Ogden's case a youth of twenty-two.

Some of the early preachers like Francis Poythress and Peter Cartwright were converted from dissipated lives into "zealous soul winners." Because they were assigned to circuits with many preaching places, these men were called "circuit riders." Their lives and histories have become associated with romance and adventure in our nation.

Here another historic Methodist word, "itineracy," should be mentioned. It originated in English Methodism. John Wesley found that the settled parish system of the English church was not effective in ministering to many groups of people. He set up a circuit plan consisting of several classes. His preachers were moved at regular intervals from one circuit to another. In America the itinerant ministry and the circuit system offered particular advantages. In the new, sparsely settled country, a single preacher could serve many societies. At first preachers were given vast circuits of one hundred or more miles around with twenty to thirty preaching points. These circuits required that they conduct services practically every day in each week.

Getting into the ranks of the itineracy required affirmative answers to four questions: (1) Is this man truly converted? (2) Does he know and keep the rules? (3) Can he preach acceptably? (4) Has he a horse? The place of the horse in the church's pioneer work forms a saga in itself. The horse was mentioned in the first *Discipline*. This is the rule preachers were required to obey: "Be merciful to your beast. Not only ride moderately but see with your eyes that your horse be rubbed and fed."

When a preacher was accepted by the annual conferences, he came under a form of discipline as stringent as any military regime. The salary promised (but not always paid) these men was sixty-four dollars per year. Between 1800-1816 the salary was eighty dollars. In 1816 it was raised to one hundred dollars.

Obviously, the life of an itinerant discouraged marriage. If a preacher did marry, it was quite certain he would soon give up traveling. In the first thirty years of the Methodist Church, 1,616 preachers were received into the conferences. During the same period approximately one half, or 821, located, most of them because of marriage.

Up until the General Conference of 1836, preachers were required to remain single until admitted to an annual conference. The policies of that day pointed toward what may be called a "Methodist celibacy." The first five bishops of the Methodist Church were bachelors. The vast majority of the preachers were single, and the rules in the *Discipline* before 1836 aimed to keep them that way. These rules provided that no preachers were to marry without consulting with their brethren. The young preachers were "to converse sparingly and cautiously with women, particularly young women." Married preachers were appointment problems, for the circuits wanted only single preachers.

The simile, "as ignorant as a Methodist preacher," an expression of contempt for uneducated circuit riders, persisted long after any justification could be had for its use. Judged from our day, the circuit riders lacked education and culture. Though they "murdered the King's English almost every lick," they were no different from the rest of the pioneers in rhetoric, dress, or manner. In fact, educationally, they ranked above the settlers.

The circuit riders often were made aware of their educational limitations by college-trained ministers of other denominations. John Strange, one of the early circuit riders in the West, gave some intimation of the kind of informal training they did possess when he boasted of being a graduate of "Brush College," a school "more ancient but less pretentious than Yale, Harvard, or Princeton." The curriculum contained such subjects as "the philosophy of nature and the mysteries of redemption"; the library contained "the word of God, the *Discipline,* and the hymn book, supplemented by trees, and brooks, and stones, all of which were full of wisdom, and sermons and speeches; and her parchments of literary honors were the horse and the saddle bags." [4]

Asbury was asked once by an educated divine from the East: "How is it that you take men from the tail of the plough, the blacksmith's shop, the carpenter's bench, and, without sending them to any college or divinity schools, set them to preach at once and in a few years they become able ministers of the New Testament, equal, if not superior, to our men trained in collegiate and theological halls?"

This was his reply: "We tell one another all we know, and then use it at once. A penny used is better than an idle dollar. You study books, we study men, the Bible, the hymn book, and Mr. Wesley's sermons, and are instant in season and out of season. I once picked up a fiddler and he became a saint and a great preacher." [5]

The circuit riders grew as they worked. Asbury set the example for study by reading as he rode. The *Discipline* called

[4] William W. Sweet, *Religion on the American Frontier,* p. 45.
[5] *History of Union County, Kentucky,* 1886.

for five hours of study daily. The earnest application many of these men made of their limited opportunities transformed them into well-educated, cultivated persons of great influence and power. Many of them became powerful preachers. They were, though, what was often called "down-to-earth" preachers; for their sermons contained both substance and nourishment.

The English preachers who were sent to America by Wesley were deeply impressed by the ability of the American itinerants. After Whatcoat and Vasey had heard some of them preach, they declared that they had not heard their equal in England with the exception of Wesley and Fletcher.

A description of the "giants of those days" from an early writer portrays them as

hardy itinerants, without education save that which most of them found in some rustic school, without any patronage derived from social position, with an entire abnegation of self and worldly prospects, with the certainty of meeting contempt and persecution at every step, with hardly "scrip or purse" for immediate necessities, cast themselves on the care and favor of God, and with only their native genius, and guided by the Spirit Divine, began a work, the greatness of which the world has not fully conceived, and the glorious end of which the world shall never see.[6]

The circuit riders were solicitous of the spiritual welfare of the immigrants, and were sympathetic with their yearnings for democracy and for economic advancement. They, like other early Americans, were independent and proud of their status as freemen. This came out frequently. On one occasion in an annual conference during a heated session, Coke rebuked the

---

[6] Scudder, *op. cit.*, p. 204.

impulsive rudeness of one of the preachers. After doing it, he asked the question, "Do you think yourselves equal to me?" Nelson Reed instantly arose and turning to Bishop Asbury, who was also present, said, "Yes, we do think ourselves equal to him, notwithstanding that he was educated at Oxford, and has been honored with the degree of Doctor of Laws; and more than that, we think ourselves equal to Dr. Coke's king." [7] The doctor remarked at the end of the statement, "He is hard upon me." Whereupon Bishop Asbury replied, "I told you that our preachers are not blockheads."

Circuit riders exemplified what may be called "muscular" Christianity. On the frontier, where they had little or no protection by law-enforcement officers, they had to look after themselves. Often meetings would be broken up by rowdies or drunken men. It was not uncommon for sinners to take the denunciations of their immoralities as personal. Peter Cartwright would not concede that "any man could whip me till it was tried." It is no idle saying that the fists of the circuit riders knocked the devil out of many sinners.

Asbury knew the regions which the preachers served. He sympathized with his men when they were tormented by ruffians. While there is no record of his directly approving the sort of muscular Christianity exemplified by such circuit riders as Peter Cartwright, on one occasion he said to a gang of rowdies: "You must remember that all our brothers in the Church are not yet sanctified, I advise you to let them alone; for if you get them angry and the devil should get in them, they are the strongest and hardest men to fight and conquer in the world. I advise you, if you do not like them, to go home and let them alone." [8]

The circuit riders under Bishop Asbury formed a mobile

[7] Garber, *op. cit.*, p. 121. Used by permission.
[8] *Ibid.*, p. 70.

force subject to his direction. When he reached America, Asbury determined that he would get the preachers out of the cities into the country where the people were. As the field marshal he sent them

where sinners were in need of the saving word. No settlement was too rundown or too remote for them. They roughed it along trails in snow and rain, taking their chances on bears, wolves, cutthroats and Indians. They put up where they could find local hospitality, which usually meant corn bread and a spot for sleeping on the dirt floor by the fire. They spent a good part of their lives hungry, wet, cold, verminous and saddlesore, and if they did not die young of consumption, they could expect an old age of rheumatism and dyspepsia.[9]

Out of 737 preachers who died before 1847, it is said that 203 were under thirty-five years of age.

Circuit riders went everywhere. They fulfilled the folk saying that in times of blizzards, snowstorms, and cloudbursts, "nobody was out but crows and Methodist preachers." Often the circuit rider's appointment would take him to where there was no sign of civilization. He would ride until he found a house and then hold services. In an old record there is the story of Richmond Nolley, a circuit rider who had traveled several days without seeing any sign of human habitation. Late in the afternoon in a remote section of Mississippi, he came upon

a fresh wagontrack. On the search for anything that had a soul, he followed it, and came upon the emigrant family just as it had pitched on the ground of the future home. The man was unlimbering his team, and the wife was busy around the fire. "What!" exclaimed the settler, upon hearing the salutation of the visitor, and taking a glance at his unmistakable appearance, "have you found me already? Another Methodist preacher! I quit Virginia to get out of reach of them; went to

[9] Bernard A. Weisberger, *They Gathered at the River* (Boston: Little, Brown and Company, 1958), p. 45. Used by permission.

71

a new settlement in Georgia, and thought to have a long whet, but they got my wife and daughter into the Church. Then, in this late purchase—Choctaw Corner—I found a piece of good land, and was sure I would have some peace of the preachers; and here is one before my wagon is unloaded."

Nolley gave him small comfort. "My friend, if you go to heaven, you'll find Methodist preachers there; and if to hell, I am afraid you'll find some there; and you see how it is in this world. So you had better make terms with us, and be at peace." [10]

The strategy used by Asbury in helping the church evangelize the young nation was to draw resources from the center to the circumference. The center of the church's work during the Revolution had shifted to Baltimore. Lines may be drawn from there to the West and the South. Soon the Western Conference (later divided into the Tennessee and Ohio conferences) became the center from which preachers were sent west to Indiana (1802), Illinois (1803), and Missouri (1806).

During the first twenty years Asbury carried responsibility for making all appointments in the United States. He was a competent judge of men and was successful in placing them where they could be most effective. He meticulously studied each recruit to the ranks. Jacob Young, a young preacher, said that when he went to the Western Conference the first time, Asbury, "his head white as a sheet," was seated at a table in the conference room writing. When Young entered, Asbury did not speak to him but raised his head, lifted his spectacles and stared, Young said, "as though he would look me through." Later just before the conference closed, Asbury called him to his room and read the account of Jacob's travels to Paddan-aram. When he came to the place where Jacob stopped for the night and

---

[10] Thomas O. Summers (ed.), *Biographical Sketches of Eminent Itinerant Ministers* (Southern Methodist Publishing House), 1859, p. 267.

took a stone for a pillow, he paused for a long time, then asked how Jacob must have felt in the lonely place. Young replied, "Very serious." Then Asbury, with this preparation, told Young he was sending him to the most difficult assignment then in the conference.

The discipline that these men accepted tells something of their own dedication to our Lord. Much could be written about their spiritual lives. Many reached a high level of saintliness. Asbury, himself a man of prayer, urged them to take time for prayer and meditation. They knelt while they prayed—any other posture was considered irreverent. Garber said the Methodist itinerants "not only covered the frontier with horseshoe prints, but left the marks of human knees wherever they crusaded." [11]

The circuit riders played a great part in helping to temper life in the new West. They had much to do with keeping the whole Western country from sinking into barbarism. At his best the circuit rider was a civilizing agent as well as a soul winner.

In an address to the General Conference of the Methodist Episcopal Church in 1908, President Theodore Roosevelt, himself an authority on the growth and development of American culture, paid this tribute to the circuit rider:

The whole country is under a debt of gratitude to the Methodist circuit riders, the Methodist pioneer preachers, whose movement westward kept pace with the movement of the frontier, who shared all the hardships in the life of that frontiersman, while at the same time ministering to that frontiersman's spiritual needs, and seeing that his pressing material cares, and the hard and grinding poverty of his life did not wholly extinguish the divine fire within his soul.

[11] *Op. cit.*, p. 82.

CHAPTER VI

The National Church
of the United States

ASBURY'S PARISH WAS THE UNITED STATES. FROM THE FIRST he planned for the Christian faith as interpreted by Methodism to be preached in every part of the country. The young Methodist Church which had identified its fortunes with the new nation was to be a national church, not a sectional one. The movement of its preachers throughout all the scattered states was, in the judgment of some historians, most helpful in unifying them.

The decision to project the ministry of the Methodist Episcopal Church to the whole nation proved to be most important for the future development of the church. Today, in several states originally settled by people from northern Europe who brought their own church with them, Methodist influence is significant. The Methodist Church in America makes a contribution to every part and segment of American life.

If the Methodist movement at the outset had followed some of the current trends, this would not have been true. When the first conference met in 1773, it was clear that the Middle and Southern colonies were most hospitable to the Wesleyan movement. Then 600 of the 1,160 members were in Virginia and Maryland. New York recorded only 132 members. During the war Methodist work declined in the Northern colonies. In 1784, New York City reported only 60 members. If the church had not purposed to be national in scope, it might have concentrated its efforts in the Southern areas while the tide was running in its favor. Instead, it moved to regain what it had lost during the war and to extend its work in the states where there were no churches. At the same time, it intensified its efforts in the South. The day after the Christmas Conference, Bishop Asbury started to Charleston, South Carolina. Soon Methodism was prospering in the parts of the country where John Wesley once had lived.

At the time of the Christmas Conference in 1784 there were no Methodist Societies in New England. Apart from a few isolated preaching excursions, the preachers had actually gone around New England, having spread into Canada and Nova Scotia on the north, to Utica and the Valley of Wyoming on the west. Appointments appeared in the conference minutes for circuits west of the Alleghenies and for settlements in the far South before New England. In 1789 at the conference held in New York, Bishop Asbury read out an appointment: Stamford—Jesse Lee. Stamford was the first town over the New York border in Connecticut. The appointment to this town really meant all of New England was to be served by the Methodists.

The reasons why Methodists had not previously formed circuits in New England are not clear. Since it was the oldest part of the country, travel throughout it would have been less difficult than in the new, unsettled sections. The explanation for its appearing on the list of appointments in 1789 points to Jesse Lee.

Asbury's appointment of Lee to New England appears to have been made with Lee's knowledge and consent. Lee had a call to the descendants of the Puritans to bestow on them some spiritual gifts which he believed their religion did not give.

When Lee traveled with Asbury in South Carolina, they stayed with a merchant in Cherow who had a clerk in his store from Massachusetts. This young man gave Lee an account of the low state of religion in New England and kindled in him a desire to go to that part of the nation to establish churches after the model of Wesleyan Societies with an Arminian theology. He was convinced that through them the formal religion of the Congregational churches could be uprooted and the errors of Calvinism corrected.

Jesse Lee at thirty-two was one of the ablest among the early Methodist itinerants. He could sing Methodist hymns in a style that left little use for the church bells to call together the congregation. McTyeire says that "his style of address was full of shrewdness as well as of force. . . . He had picked up a little colloquial Dutch; and when to test his scholarship the parsons and school-masters, full of Greek and Latin, addressed him in an unknown tongue, he paid them back in their own coin." [1]

Lee preached the first Methodist sermon in Boston, standing on a table on historic Boston Common. He organized the first Methodist Church in New England at Stratfield, Connecticut, September 26, 1789. In the eight years he spent in New England he touched every part and laid down foundations for the church. Of his labors someone remarked, "In a soil so hard and temperature so low, the cause was slow in taking root." The records show that the first classes were small, often only two or three persons. The church grew in spite of persecution. Converts were won at the rate of 500 a year. At the end of the second decade Methodist membership in New England was 14,488.

The Congregational Church, from the time of the "Mayflower," had been the dominating church of New England.

[1] *Op. cit.,* pp. 420, 421.

New England knew of the Methodists and had formed some conclusions about them. In fact, to the rigid adherents of Calvinism, Methodism was synonymous with fanaticism and heresy. Methodist preachers were considered uncouth and ignorant. Congregationalists required of their pastors a college education. Almost all the preachers in New England then were college trained. When Jesse Lee crossed into Connecticut and applied for lodging at an inn, he told the hostess he was a preacher and expected to preach in the village. She promptly asked, "Have you a liberal education, sir?" Lee answered, "Tolerable, madam; enough, I think, to carry me through the country." [2]

New Englanders associated the extemporaneous preaching of Methodists with a lack of education. They assumed that an educated preacher showed both his erudition and preparation by reading his sermon from a manuscript.

The clergymen were the ruling class in secular as well as religious affairs. No one could hold office in any of these states unless he was a member in good standing of a Congregational church. They resented the presence of the Methodist preachers and charged them with disturbing the religious life of the people. One of their preachers told Thomas Ware, a Methodist itinerant, that "you make people commit sin in the loss of so much precious time as is wasted in attending your meetings on week days when they ought to be at labor; or on the Sabbath in leaving the places where they ought to worship to run after you." [3]

Along with public roads and public schools the churches in Massachusetts, Connecticut, and New Hampshire then were supported through taxes. This meant that the living for the

[2] *Ibid.*, 421.
[3] *Ibid.*, p. 127.

clergymen was paid by taxes collected from often unwilling parishioners. All persons were subject to this tax unless they could show that they were supporting some religious organization other than "the standing order."

When the first Methodist Society was started in Lynn, Massachusetts, in 1790, Lee says that "upwards of seventy men, who paid tax, came together and took certificates shewing that they attended public worship with the Methodists, and paid to the support of their minister." [4]

On the surface it may seem that the opposition of the established church to Methodism was for the protection of their theology and dogma, but lurking in the background was the threat that a free church brought to parish revenues.

On his visits to New England, Asbury found it "socially and religiously inhospitable." In 1794, he wrote that the states were "fettered with ecclesiastical chains—taxed to support the ministers, who are chosen by a small committee, and settled for life. . . . O what a happy people would these be if they were not thus priest-ridden." [5]

This difficult field was another one of the "train of providences" mentioned by early Methodists. In New England, Methodist preachers faced college-trained ministers who were intellectually able to state and defend their theological principles. Consequently, Methodist preachers of necessity had to understand their own doctrine, and this called for careful study of anti-Calvinistic writings. This may furnish an explanation of why at the outset so many of Methodism's ablest leaders came from New England. The six most prominent and creative leaders selected by Bishop Matthew Simpson as bringing strength and power to the Methodist movement during the first part of

[4] Quoted in Sweet, *Methodism in American History,* p. 125.
[5] *The Journal and Letters,* II, 22.

the nineteenth century included five from New England—Joshua Soule, Nathan Bangs, Wilbur Fisk, Elijah Hedding, and Martin Ruter. The sixth one was John Emory.

When there were only about eight thousand Methodists in New England, the conference decided that a school was necessary. Methodist children who were sent to the schools run by the established churches were in most instances lost to the church. Schools then were effective proselyting agencies. In 1817 Methodists opened an academy at Newmarket, New Hampshire. Out of this small beginning, however, Wilbraham Academy and Wesleyan University were to emerge.

One contribution of Methodism to New England which is often overlooked was the impetus furnished in humanizing the Calvinistic theology of that region. In that period of reaction from the stern Calvinism of the Puritans to Unitarianism the reasonable evangelical position of Methodism was needed by persons who, sincerely desiring to be Christians, could not accept the teachings of either Calvinism or Unitarianism.

Before the War of 1812 Methodist work in Canada was administered by the Methodist Episcopal Church in the United States. At the end of hostilities, American Methodists found that the Canadian authorities were more kindly disposed toward the Methodist preachers from England. In 1824 the work was turned over to the Canadian Methodist Episcopal Church. It ceased to be part of the Methodist Episcopal Church in the United States.

The section of the United States in which Methodist pioneering was to be most fruitful was the Mississippi Valley. The story of its settlement forms one of the most dramatic stories in American history. The reports made by Daniel Boone and other adventurers stirred the desires of people, most of whom had migrated from their native lands to acquire land of their own. Boone told of a country beyond the mountains where the meadows and woodlands stretched as far as the eye could see. Game abounded there—buffalo, bear, turkey—so plentiful that the hunter could kill as fast as he could load and fire.

The way there was over the Wilderness Road, which started near Philadelphia and ran through Cumberland Gap, Virginia. This was one of the most important thoroughfares of the world. Yet to travel it was a dangerous adventure. In 1790 Asbury rode it, but not without caution. He had seen signs of Indian massacres. At a point not far from the present town of Barbourville, Kentucky, he stood guard while the company with which he was traveling slept. "I saw the bodies of the slain," Asbury wrote, "twenty-four in one camp. I learned that they had set no guards, and . . . the Indians came upon the camp." Asbury's report of this country confirms Boone's. He called it the richest body of fertile soil he had ever beheld.[6]

In 1790 when the first census was taken, there were about four million people in the United States. In spite of the hazards, immigrations to the West increased, so that between the years of 1790 and 1820, ten new states west of the Alleghenies were added to the Union.

So fast had been the movement of people westward during these thirty years that the older states were alarmed at their loss of population. From the beginning of the War of 1812 to 1920 occurred the greatest movement of population ever witnessed in America. The roads westward swarmed with wagons, cattle, sheep, and horses. Even throughout the winter months sleighs loaded with women, children, and household goods were to be seen on their way to Ohio and the West. All America, said a European observer, seems to be breaking up and moving westward.[7]

[6] *Journal and Letters*, I, 636-37.
[7] Sweet, *op. cit.*, p. 117.

In 1786 at the conference meeting in Baltimore, James Haw and Benjamin Ogden were sent to a new circuit called "Kentucky." A missionary offering was taken for money to bear their expenses to the new charge. The Kentucky circuit then included Tennessee, and Benjamin Ogden organized the first societies in that state. Benjamin Wofford, founder of Wofford College, once rode a circuit which "embraced Central Kentucky and Middle Tennessee." It was bounded on the north by the Ohio River, on the east by the Cumberland Mountains, and on the south and west in a general way by the Tennessee River.[8] The first permanent settlements were in this region. Methodist preachers came with the pioneers to establish churches.

Kentucky is not to be considered merely as a circuit. It became the gateway through which pioneer preachers moved farther to the West and to the South. Prior to 1821, the date of the formation of the Kentucky Conference, Kentucky was included in the Western Conference. This conference also organized the first circuits in Ohio in 1798, Indiana, 1802, Illinois, 1803, and Missouri, 1806. Included also was the vast area on the lower Mississippi River.

Tobias Gibson, who opened the work of the church in the Southwest, had to cross the mountains into Tennessee to start his journey by boat. A native of Georgia, he was reported to have had considerable wealth. Impressed with a strong desire to visit Natchez, he offered himself to Bishop Asbury as a missionary to this region. The starting point was Pedee, South Carolina, from which he made his way six hundred miles through the wilderness and over mountains to the Cumberland River at some point in Tennessee. Arriving at the river, he sold his horse, bought a canoe, paddled down the Cumberland River

---

[8] Cullen Carter, *Methodism in the Wilderness* (Nashville: Parthenon Press), p. 15.

to the Ohio, down the Ohio to the Mississippi, and on to Natchez. Gibson's work covered the whole region reaching from Florida on the east to Natchez on the west. Later it was to move southward to New Orleans and westward to the Red River regions of Louisiana.

The church did grow with the nation. In 1800 there were 2,801 members in the whole West. By 1812 there were 30,741 who claimed membership. In 1830 the original Western Conference had grown to eight with a membership of more than 175,000. That is a growth of 172,199 in thirty years.[9]

When the Christmas Conference met in 1784 it was difficult to find a Methodist, but in 1810 there was one Methodist for every thirty-nine persons in America. In 1840, one out of every nineteen in the nation was a Methodist. The population increased 36 per cent between 1800 and 1810, while Methodism increased 36 per cent during the same period. The growth of Methodism between 1800 and 1830 was sevenfold. The Methodist Church soon became the largest Protestant group in America, and by 1860 one third of American Protestants were Methodist.

One aspect of the religious development of the West was the spiritual awakening between 1797 and 1805. This was especially important because the results of it were carried by the pioneers beyond the Ohio. The revival was not Methodist in origin, but Presbyterian. Methodists joined the Presbyterians in the movement and profited from it.

One facet of the revival, the camp meeting, became a part of religious folklore of America. In a special way the camp meeting met the religious and social needs of the sparsely settled frontier. People came from forty or fifty miles to some central place.

[9] William W. Sweet, *The Story of Religion in America* (2nd ed.; New York: Harper & Brothers, 1930), p. 220-21.

Ten, twenty, and sometimes thirty preachers were present and services were conducted several times during the day. In some camp meetings there were several simultaneous services.

The camp meetings are often remembered because of their emotional excesses. The meetings were accompanied by bodily agitations such as jerking, rolling, dancing, and barking. The falling exercise had appeared in Methodist revivals in both England and America. Persons stricken by conviction of sin would fall to the floor and lie as if dead until revived. Peter Cartwright, who was a great camp-meeting preacher, said he had seen more than a hundred sinners fall like dead men under one powerful sermon.

The strange phenomenon of these camp-meeting revivals, which caused no small amazement, was a nervous physical condition known as the "jerks." When the "jerks" would break over an audience, saints and sinners alike would be swayed by them.

Barton Stone, one of the founders of the Disciples of Christ, who led in the Cane Ridge Camp Meeting in 1797, gives a first-hand account of the "jerks."

Sometimes the subject of the jerks would be affected in some one member of the body, and sometimes the whole system. When the head alone was affected, it would be jerked backward and forward or from side to side so quickly that the features of the face could not be distinguished. When the whole system was affected, I have seen the person, stand in one place, and jerk backward and forward in quick succession, the head nearly touching the floor behind and before. . . . I have seen wicked persons thus affected and all the time cursing the jerks while they were thrown to the earth with violence. Though so awful to behold, I do not remember that any one of the thousands I have seen ever sustained an injury in body.

These meetings drew immense congregations and "were composed both of worshipers and of numbers of families who came merely to enjoy the show. When several hundred lonely men and women were brought together for three or four days in an informal outdoor setting, nature took its course among the awakened and unredeemed alike." [10]

The religious revivals and the ministrations of the early Methodist preachers to the people in the new West were important influences in their social and cultural growth. Life there was drab. The books and other aids needed for the enrichment of the people were not available to the vast majority of the first settlers. Gerald W. Johnson, a student of the cultural development of early America, credits the hymns of Charles Wesley and Isaac Watts with doing "more toward determining the early American's attitude toward the art than was done by Johann Sebastian Bach, who, if he was known to Americans at all, was known only through some fragment of his music attached to the words by Wesley or Watts." [11]

Often students of American life blame Methodism's plain and simple forms of worship for the artistic sterility of its people for many generations. Such a criticism fails to evaluate the conditions under which the church began its work.

An esthetically barren environment must inevitably influence people to turn to a religion as little as possible dependent upon such adornments; as color, music, and rhythm. The severely rationalistic doctrine of the Methodists, far from reflecting beauty, instructed its adherents that the richest liturgy is but a faint representation of the spiritual beauty that is the truth of the believer's quest. The pioneers and their successors for generations lived in an environment in which the amenities of civilization had to wait upon the necessities of survival.[12]

[10] Weisberger, op. cit., p. 36. Used by permission.
[11] Gerald W. Johnson, Our English Heritage (Philadelphia: J. B. Lippincott Company, 1949), p. 190.
[12] Weisberger, op. cit., p. 174 ff.

"Spreading the seeds of eternal life" did not mean that the builders of the church lacked concern about the development of the new nation. The preachers considered themselves "Americanizing agents" and Alexis de Tocqueville called them "missionaries of Christian civilization." De Tocqueville also observed that Christianity was considered to be indispensable to the maintenance of republican government.

Early Methodism made a distinct contribution to pioneer America by helping the people to develop the moral and character qualities needed for citizenship in the new republic. Public morals could not be made dependent upon law-enforcement agencies. They had to result from the integrity of the people. While Methodist preachers readily associated religious faith with political democracy, they never assumed that democracy in itself could be a substitute for the Christian religion.

Early Methodism appealed to the people who were at the bottom of the social ladder. Through a religious awakening many showed a desire for both self-improvement and service to mankind. The organization of the Methodist Episcopal Church was geared to help them. The class meeting gave opportunities for public speaking. Some who became leaders on the new frontier were individuals who got their training in these meetings. Notable among them was the first governor of Ohio, Edwin Tiffin, who was licensed to preach. Because he was married and had a family, Tiffin did not enter the itineracy. As a citizen of Ohio, he was elected to the convention which formed the state constitution. He became Ohio's first governor and later a member of the United States Senate.

America was idealized by its founders as a land in which every man would have opportunity to develop without respect to social grades or other differences. That hope has come nearer to being realized here than in any other part of the world. Religious faith explains why this experiment succeeded here. The Methodist movement, with its deep passion for personal religious experience, individual freedom, and initiative, made in its own unique way significant contributions to the fulfillment of the dream.

CHAPTER VII

Publish Good News

WHILE JOHN WESLEY'S NAME IS USUALLY ASSOCIATED WITH preaching, he is also remembered as a prolific author and publisher. Someone remarked of him that "he read so much his friends were unable to see how he could find any time to write, and he wrote so much that they could not discover how he could find any time to read." [1] During his lifetime he prepared 371 publications covering an enormous range of subjects, including dictionaries and textbooks for Kingswood School and working libraries for preachers.

It is not possible to appreciate fully the Methodist movement apart from the literature—tracts, books, papers—that it produced and circulated. The literature was diversified. It included devotional, expository, and inspirational materials. For the benefit of underprivileged converts, selections of the best of established writings were published in inexpensive bindings. Wesley's interests encompassed the whole person, head as well as heart. In moving men and women into right ways of thinking, his publications helped to improve the character of not only his generation but others which followed.

The Methodist movement, Henry Bett said,

lifted millions from a life of ignorance and brutality and made them intelligent and responsible men; it gave them some interest in books and music, if only at first in religious books and sacred music. Many

[1] F. M. Larkin, *One Hundred Years of Progress*, 1820-1920 (Cincinnati: The Methodist Book Concern), p. 43.

a man who would otherwise have been a mere brute was brought first of all to an experience of religion and led to study his Bible and read some of the books written by Wesley or recommended by him to his people.

The first Methodists in this country needed the same kind of help from the printed pages as did English Methodists. Preachers who could leave a tract or leaflet in a home started an influence which would outlast a sermon. They learned from experience that Wesley's publications served the interests of truth and piety. Asbury and Dickins were especially eager to find some way to provide suitable literature for the societies.

The founding of the Methodist Book Concern marks an epoch in both the religious and cultural advance of our nation. It showed that the Methodists believed that edification and salvation belong together. The Book Concern, Henry C. Jennings, one of its publishing agents, said, combined book concern with soul concern. The name chosen for the new organization at any rate indicated this idea was not foreign to the mind of the founders. The Methodist printing enterprise did exercise a beneficent influence upon the culture as well as upon the religion of the new country.

We have often said that the religious revivals and labors of Methodist preachers definitely aided in establishing a civilized way of life in the new country. This is a fact of history and acknowledged by secular historians.

Self-education through reading was a definite part of the civilizing program. The long list of books—Bibles, hymnals, *Disciplines,* and other books—which were sold by the circuit riders furnished a vast amount of religious instruction to the people on the frontier. Lewis B. Wright, an authority on the history of the West, said, "The circuit rider, as a book agent, as a carrier of letters and learning, even on the modest level that his own background and the capacity of his saddlebags would provide, is a theme worthy of our respect and our study. This dissemination of books in the west became a peculiar occupation of Methodists."

The fountainhead of this self-education movement was the Methodist Book Concern. Its growth and influence may be attributed to its having the support of the whole church. "Connectional" is a historic Methodist expression, and the church often is called a "connectional" one. The term signifies that all its churches and enterprises are connected through a central organization. This makes it possible for the General Conference to project plans and programs for all the conferences and churches. The Book Concern became the first church-wide agency of the many which would be set up as the church grew. Its life and service has been to the whole church.

The date recognized for the founding of the publishing enterprise was 1789. This does not mean that Methodists waited until that time to start the use of the printed page in their work. There is a touch of irony in the fact that the Methodist preacher Robert Williams,[2] whom Wesley unwillingly consented to appoint to America, should turn out to be the first of his missionaries to circulate Wesley's own literature. Williams brought with him some copies of Wesley's sermons. The demand for them soon exhausted his supply. Williams then, on his own initiative, had more printed. When Wesley heard that Williams was doing this, he wrote Asbury to put a stop to it. Apparently the objection was because, as Asbury noted, "it was for the sake of gain." "This," Asbury added, "will not do. It does not look well."

On July 11, 1773, the Conference put an end to Robert

[2] See Ch. III.

Williams' career as a publisher of Methodist materials. It declared that "no preacher shall be permitted to reprint our books, without the approbation of Mr. Wesley and the consent of his brethren. And that Robert Williams shall be allowed to sell what he has, but reprint no more.[3]

Adverse judgment must not be passed on Robert Williams for his zeal in publishing Methodist literature. Jesse Lee, in commenting on the work of Williams, justifies the Conference's action by saying it was "necessary for the preachers to be all united in the same cause of printing and selling our books so that the profits arising therefrom, might be divided among the preachers or applied to some charitable purpose."

Williams was a devoted Christian and effective Methodist preacher. He was influential in planting the church in parts of Maryland and Virginia. The tracts and sermons that he distributed had far-reaching results. One of the ablest of the early American Methodist preachers, Philip Gatch, a pioneer in the Northwest Territory and one of the writers of Ohio's constitution,[4] was converted after reading Wesley's sermon on "Salvation by Faith," that had been printed by Williams. Asbury paid this tribute to Williams: "He has been a very useful, laborious man, and the Lord gave him many seals to his ministry. Perhaps no one in America has been an instrument of awakening so many souls as God has awakened by him."

Lee's and Asbury's observations show that at the very beginning of The Methodist Church the printing and selling of Christian literature was to be under church control. No one was to do it for private profit.

[3] *Journal and Letters of Francis Asbury,* I, 85.
[4] See Paul H. Boase, "Philip Gatch: He Helped Save Methodism," *The Christian Advocate* (March 3, 1960), pp. 7-8.

The Christmas Conference of 1784 expressed the importance of the church's circulating religious literature, especially Wesley's writings. Preachers were to keep all the societies supplied with books. The three books recommended there were *The Christian Pattern*, a translation by Wesley of Thomas a Kempis' *Imitation of Christ; Instructions for Children;* and *Primitive Physic* by Wesley. The books mentioned in 1784 had special significance to Methodists of that day. The first one suggested their effort to spread holiness throughout the continent; the second reflected the importance of the religious nurture of children, and the last, apparently, was regarded as a household medical guide needed by pioneers isolated from physicians.

In the Conference of 1789, held in New York, the handicaps of not having some centralized, systematic plan for publishing the literature needed for the church was again lamented. The main obstacle had been the lack of money to get the work under way. Here a name previously mentioned in the unfolding story of early Methodism comes again to the forefront—John Dickins. At a critical point in the discussion of the importance of getting the work going, he spoke up and said: "Brethren, be of good cheer; I have one hundred and twenty pounds sterling [about six hundred dollars], the savings of my lifetime. I will loan every cent of it to the Methodist Book Concern for the establishment of a Publishing House to carry forward the gospel of Jesus Christ by the printed page." [5]

Born in 1747 in London and educated at Eton, one of England's best-known schools, Dickins became a Methodist after migrating to America in 1774 and entered the itinerant ministry in 1777. Asbury wrote in his journal that John Dickins was "a man of great piety, great skill in learning, drinks in

[5] Larkin, *op. cit.,* p. 77.

Greek and Latin swiftly; yet prays much, and walks close with God." [6] Dickins' creative and imaginative leadership made him one of the most important personalities in establishing the Methodist Episcopal Church on solid ground. While he is connected with many "firsts" in America, including the college to which he was the first contributor, his name is intimately linked with the publishing enterprise.

Since the Methodist Episcopal Church then did not have another church-wide meeting after 1784 until 1792, the decisions on church policies and plans rested with the annual conferences. Eleven of these were held in 1789. It may be surmised that in each one the need for a publishing agency was discussed. However, it remained for the annual conference meeting in New York to take final action on the program. This conference, which formally set up the Methodist Book Concern, had nineteen preachers present, including Bishops Coke and Asbury. The action, Bishop Coke said, assured Methodists of a supply of books of "pure divinity for their reading which is of the next importance to preaching."

The *Discipline* published following this conference contained the following directives for the Book Concern:

As it has been frequently recommended by the preachers and people, that such books as are wanted, be printed in this country, we therefore propose,

(1) that the advice of the conference shall be desired concerning any valuable impression and their consent be obtained before any steps be taken for the printing thereof.

(2) that the profits of the books, after all the necessary expenses are defrayed, shall be applied, according to the discretion of the con-

[6] *Journal and Letters,* I, 358.

ference, towards the college, the preachers' fund, the deficiencies of the preachers the distant missions, or the debts on our churches.

The conference vested responsibility for launching the publishing work with the man who loaned the church the money. John Dickins was moved from New York to Philadelphia to serve as pastor of St. George's Church and to get the work under way. Phillip Cox was named by that conference as "book steward." He was left without a charge in order to give full time as a colporteur. This seems to be the first "special appointment" made by Asbury. It released a preacher from circuit work in order that he might be free to push the sale of the church's publications.

The first book published in the United States after the organization of the Methodist Book Concern was a reprint of John Wesley's abridgment and translation from the Latin of Thomas a Kempis' *Imitation of Christ,* named *The Christian Pattern.* Following this came a new edition of the Methodist *Discipline* and Richard Baxter's *Saints' Everlasting Rest.* Later came John Fletcher's answer to Calvinism known as *Checks to Antinomianism.* This book indicates that the Methodists had taken the initiative against Calvinism in behalf of unlimited redemption. It showed that they intended to oppose vigorously its teaching. This was followed by the printing of a magazine bearing the title, *The Arminian Magazine.* These materials helped to set the direction for the development of Methodist theology in the United States.

John Dickins' leadership of the Methodist publishing interest continued until his death in 1798. An unpublished manuscript by J. Minton Batten on "The History of the Methodist Publishing House" outlines the duties of the first publishing agent. Dickins "planned the publication program, wrote some of the

93

materials published, edited the manuscripts, granted printing contracts and checked their fulfillment, read proof, ran the bookstore or depository in Philadelphia, packed books for shipment, kept accounts, and exercised supervisory jurisdiction over the work of the traveling book steward." When he had some leisure from the above duties, Batten said, Dickins would pack the top of his tall stovepipe hat with Methodist literature and go out on the streets of Philadelphia and sell his publications, using his hat as a display case.

The assets of the Book Concern at the time of Dickins' death in 1798 were $4,000 and its liabilities were $4,500. This deficit came partly from granting Cokesbury College $800 out of profits before they were earned. In fact, the financial difficulties of the Book Concern usually were the result of appropriating anticipated earnings to charities and other organizations such as Cokesbury College, missions, and schools for the Indians. Such practices, if not curtailed, would mean inevitable bankruptcy for the new undertaking. At the General Conference of 1804 all profits of the Book Concern were designated for the support of the distressed traveling preachers and their widows and orphans.

This step marks the beginning of one phase of the Publishing House's operations that has proved to be significant in the life of the church. In 1808 when the charter of the Methodist Episcopal Church was adopted, one of the six restrictive regulations provided that the General Conference "shall not appropriate the produce of the book concern nor of the chartered fund to any purpose other than for the benefit of the traveling, supernumerary, superannuated and worn-out preachers, their wives, widows, and children."

This policy has been followed from 1808 to the present. Since that date the annual conferences of The Methodist Church have received in dividends—up until 1959—more than seventeen million dollars. Grants now are beyond one-half million annually. The success of Methodist publishing has been intimately related to the agents it has chosen. Ezekiel Cooper succeeded Dickins. He faced a discouraging task with the insolvent enterprise and only through pressure from Bishop Asbury did he agree to serve. His genius as a businessman is seen in his report to the General Conference of 1804. It showed that all debts had been paid and a working capital of $57,000 had been accumulated. Cooper was assisted for a while by Asbury Dickins, a son of John D. Dickins, who later was made secretary of the United States Senate and served from 1836 to 1861. Other agents of the early period were Joshua Soule, Nathan Bangs, and John Emory.

The growth of the church in the West and South prompted the General Conference of 1820 to locate a branch of the Book Concern in Cincinnati. The Mississippi valley was being settled rapidly. The church's publications needed to be more accessible. Martin Ruter, who had served as pastor of the "Methodist Cathedral" of Philadelphia, St. George's, and as the president of the first school in New England, was elected the book agent for Cincinnati. It often has been said that big men do not despise small things if they see their significance and meaning. This must have been true of Ruter. His place of business in Cincinnati was a room fifteen by twenty feet. He himself made up the entire working force of the business from errand boy to manager.

The selection of Cincinnati as the location of the Western branch proved to be a wise choice. Cincinnati then was the most important cultural center in the West and South. For many years it led the nation in the publication of textbooks for schools. This country west of the mountains called for more optimistic books for their schools than the ones produced by the New England publishers. Ruter sensed this demand for publications for the public schools and prepared several books, including *The New Spelling Book, The New American Primer, An Arithmetic,* and the *Juvenile Preceptor.*

William Holmes McGuffey, the person who was to exert the greatest influence upon making the mind of America during the nineteenth century, was located not far from Cincinnati during the early years of the Western branch. The famous readers which became the texts for America's schools for almost a century were published in Cincinnati. These swept the western and southern part of the nation. They remained in use during the balance of the nineteenth century. More than 122,000,000 copies of these books were published in Cincinnati. Their continuous impact upon the minds of millions of young Americans constructively influenced their moral, religious, and cultural growth. When the South was cut off during the war from access to Cincinnati, the Methodist Book Concern of Nashville printed the *McGuffey Readers* and supplied the region west and south of Nashville.[7]

A news story which summarizes the current work of the Methodist Publishing House in 1958 tells of the mighty stream of religious literature which flows from that organization in a single year: 4,800,000 hard-bound books; 120,000,000 pieces of church-school materials; 900,000 copies of *Together,* the church's family religious magazine. In printing these publications, 30,000,000 pounds of paper are used and 255,000 pounds of printers' ink. The sale of books and publications reaches $25,000,000 annually. From the profits, $600,000 go to the Methodist conferences for their retired ministers, and widows and orphans of deceased ministers.

[7] Henry H. Vial, *History of McGuffey Readers* (Cleveland, Ohio: Burrows Brothers Company, 1911), p. 53.

This summary of one year of the life of the publishing program of the church shows something of its present proportions. But who can delineate what it has meant to the spread of our Christian faith throughout the world since its founding in 1789? The millions and millions of pages of books, *Christian Advocates*, Sunday-school papers, and tracts brought spiritual inspiration and educational advance to literally millions of people. We should be grateful that actual poverty did not prevent our church fathers from seeing the possibilities of a publishing ministry. The Methodist Publishing House has become one of Christendom's greatest enterprises for the production of Christian literature. And it all began with a loan of six hundred dollars.

CHAPTER VIII

Help for the Needy
—Missionary Beginnings

FROM ITS BEGINNING, THE METHODIST CHURCH HAS BEEN a missionary and evangelistic movement, even though our Methodist fathers did not use these two words to describe their work. Their thoughts were not on settled parishes but on the "lost sheep of the Church of England," and the unchurched masses on the frontier. Umphrey Lee said, "At the beginning of the last century so fixed was the notion that Methodism was a missionary movement that the proposal to organize a missionary society in the Methodist church in the United States was opposed by many on the ground that the church itself was a missionary movement." [1]

Every special concern now epitomized in some national church board, such as education, publishing, temperance, may be traced to the first days of the Methodist movement. "The Book of Methodism," Bishop Nolan B. Harmon says, became not a prayer book but a discipline—"not *ordered worship* but *ordered life and activity*." [2] In no sense should the date of a board's organization mean the time of the church's interest in that special cause. It only means that an agency was set up to widen the local church's reach in its effort to further a historic emphasis.

[1] *Our Fathers and Us* (Dallas, Tex.: Southern Methodist University Press, 1958), p. 3.
[2] *The Rites and Ritual of Episcopal Methodism* (Nashville: Publishing House of the M. E. Church, South, 1926), p. 48.

The gospel preached by John Wesley called for help to the people in need. Wesley's interpretation of the gospel aroused social concern and prompted action. In brief, religion "called for doing good unto all men." The services thus inspired covered a variety of needs. Clothing was distributed to the poor and help was provided for the incapacitated and unemployed. Loans were made available to small businessmen and persons unable to qualify for credit at banks. A dispensary was provided for medical aid to the indigent sick. Schools were organized for children excluded from the few schools of that day. A study of these and other services shows that Wesley anticipated the sort of services which an organized social ministry in later years was to render. What Woodrow Wilson said of Wesley has been true of the church he founded: "Everything he touched took shape as if with a new sort of institutional life."

The concern for persons gave Methodism a passion for carrying the gospel to any neglected people. Asbury accepted his appointment from Wesley to missionary service. Through the forty-five years he thought of himself as a missionary. The circuit riders were Asbury's missionaries. Jesse Lee's interest in New England caused him to offer himself as a missionary to that region. In 1798 John Kobler was sent by Bishop Asbury as a missionary to Ohio, a country where no sound of the everlasting gospel had broken upon the people's ears or gladdened their hearts.

The assignments made to Methodist itinerants constituted at that time what some other churches termed "domestic missions." The Methodist preachers' complete identification with the people to whom they were sent made the term "missionary" incongruous. But it was missionary work on the highest level. As Stephen Olin, the first president of Randolph-Macon College, observed, it "saved the whole region west and southwest of the Allegheny mountains from the ineffable curse of our infidel and semi-heathen population."

The forming of missionary societies in Protestant churches began during the last part of the eighteenth century and the first decades of the nineteenth century. Up until then they had been indifferent to work beyond their own parishes. This is remembered in connection with William Carey's call to send missionaries to India. To Carey's plea the chairman shouted, "Sit down, young man. When God pleases to convert the heathen, He will do it without your aid or mine."

The missionary activities of Protestant churches in the United States during the eighteenth century had been limited to the Indians and the migrants moving into the new West. One of the first organized attempts to arouse concern for foreign missions was led by a group of students at Williams College in Massachusetts. The story of it begins with the so-called "Haystack" [3] prayer meeting. Five students had gone to the field for prayer. A rain drove them to seek shelter in a haystack. While there, they resolved to dedicate their efforts to convince the church of its responsibility for foreign missions. Out of this movement came America's first missionary society, the American Board of Commissioners for Foreign Missions, founded in 1810. Other groups followed in setting up societies. The established churches in America, however, continued to be indifferent to foreign work, often regarding the agitation as "overheated religious zeal and fanaticism."

While the Methodists did not organize a missionary society until 1819, missions were included as an emphasis in the Christmas Conference. At this conference, two preachers, Freeborn Garrettson and James O. Cromwell, in answer to an earnest plea

[3] Clarence P. Shedd, *Two Centuries of Student Christian Movements* (New York: Association Press, 1934), p. 51.

made by William Black, a local preacher from Nova Scotia, were sent to that province. According to the Methodist historian, Abel Stevens, these were the first missionaries sent beyond the borders of the United States by a Protestant church.

Without question, the first concern in the Methodist Episcopal Church for foreign missions was planted by Thomas Coke. In 1784, eight years before William Carey went to India, Coke published a tract on "A Plan of the Society for the Establishment of Missions Among the Heathens." It is believed that it was through his urging that the Christmas Conference responded to the appeal made by William Black to send missionaries to Nova Scotia. This work was regarded then as "foreign missions." Coke personally assumed responsibility for financing the work. He raised the funds needed at the Christmas Conference and from solicitations made in Baltimore, Philadelphia, and New York.

This missionary concern for Nova Scotia later was the indirect cause for starting a mission in the West Indies. When Coke returned to England, he recruited through Wesley's help three additional missionaries for Nova Scotia, but the ship on which Coke and the three missionaries sailed for Nova Scotia was driven off its course by storms and landed instead at St. John's on the island of Antigua on Christmas Day.

Here they found that Methodist work had been started by a man named Nathaniel Gilbert, who on a visit to England had been converted by John Wesley. Upon his return Gilbert began preaching to his slaves. He formed them into classes. Later, John Baxter, a local preacher who had been sent to work as a shipwright to the British fleet at Antigua, took over the work.

The story of the evangelization of Antigua greatly stirred Coke. He found that the island had been completely transformed under the preaching of Gilbert and Baxter. Before they started the work, martial law had to be proclaimed at Christmas to control the drunken excesses. With the coming of Methodism, this was no longer needed. Methodist chapels had supplanted the need of law enforcement.

Fortunately for the American Methodists, Coke's interests were directed toward missions. He never learned to understand the Methodist preachers of the New World. Furthermore, Coke never had the same sense of dedication to America as Asbury. He continued to maintain close ties with Wesley and English Methodists. It was assumed by many that he would be Wesley's successor. But fortunately for Methodist missionary work, English Methodist preachers had other designs.

Coke united the first missionary efforts of American and English Methodists. It was in England, however, that he laid his broad plans for carrying the gospel to other lands. He served as president of the Missionary Committee. With his own funds he financed the beginnings of Methodist missionary work in Africa. India became the center of his concern. He wrote to Wilberforce that he would give up all to go there. "Could I but close my life in being the means of raising up a spiritual Church in India, it would satisfy the utmost ambition of my soul here." [4] While a way for a mission to India could not be opened, the conference did accept his proposal for one to the Far East. On December 31, 1813, Coke, along with a contingent of missionaries, sailed for Ceylon, Java, and the Cape of Good Hope. On May 3, 1814, while en route, Coke died. He was buried at sea.

Coke can be called Methodism's first great missionary statesman. The work he started grew in importance and influence. To the missionary program launched by English Methodists in India, Coke had advanced his own money for the work. His account

---

[4] Warren A. Candler, *Life of Thomas Coke* (Nashville: Publishing House of the Methodist Episcopal Church, South, 1923), pp. 370-72.

in 1793 showed that "he had lent 11,000 pounds (about $30,800 in American money) to the work, none of which was repaid." [5]

The first missionary work of American Methodists was limited to the neglected parts of North America. This in part may have resulted from the limited financial resources of American Methodists. Even to pay their own preachers as much as eighty dollars per year, Methodists had to make gifts in "kind," such as clothing, along with cash. During Asbury's last years, he "carried about a subscription book, in which no one was allowed to subscribe more than one dollar. This he called his mite subscription, and the sums collected were divided among the annual conferences to meet the most needy cases.[6] The heathen the first Methodist missionaries set out to reach were found in Canada and among the Indians, the slaves, and the destitute.

The man who is credited with starting American Methodism's first missionary activity was John Stewart, who had both Negro and Indian blood in his veins. Under the preaching of Marcus Lindsey he had been soundly converted in Ohio from a dissolute life. Soon after he embraced religion, he went into the fields to pray. "It seemed to me," he said, "that I heard a voice like the voice of a woman praising God and then another as the voice of a man saying to me, 'You must declare my counsel faithfully.' These voices ran through me powerfully. They seemed to come to me from a northwest direction. This circumstance made a strong impression on my mind and seemed an indication to me that the Lord had called me to warn sinners to flee the wrath to come." [7]

In following this call from the northwest, Stewart finally

[5] Umphrey Lee and William W. Sweet, *A Short History of Methodism* (Nashville: Abingdon Press, 1956), p. 64.

[6] William W. Sweet, *Circuit Rider Days Along the Ohio*, p. 70.

[7] Wade Crawford Barclay, *Early American Methodism* (Nashville: Board of Missions of The Methodist Church, 1949-50), I, 204.

reached the Delaware Indians. He announced a service. Only one Indian—a squaw—came to it. It is said that he preached as earnestly to her as to an audience of a thousand. Crowds soon came and conversions followed, including those of several influential chiefs.

Stewart's success made a profound impression upon the church. It sounded a call to more vigorous missionary work. In 1819, the Ohio Annual Conference authorized a mission to the Wyandot Indians—the first official one made by the Methodist Episcopal Church to the Indians. The development of this work later under James B. Finley forms an epic in missionary annals.

The first missionary society in the Methodist Episcopal Church was organized in 1819. Since there were a number of independent societies in existence, it became necessary that the whole be centralized and made a connectional enterprise. The first society was not an immediate success. It was only after considerable effort by a number of people, among them Nathan Bangs, that the society was able to arouse and sustain interest. Many believed that churches should give priority to their own needs. However, two movements of the eighteenth century contributed to its development: an awakened concern for the ignorant and suffering among Christians, and the explorations being made in foreign lands.

The General Conference of 1820 provided for a missionary society. Following its action, the way was opened for one of the greatest periods of expansion known in the church. The new society at its beginning lifted the sights of the church from beyond the routine responsibilities of the local churches to wider challenges. These included the French of Louisiana, who needed "the unadulterated Word," the Spanish in Florida, and the wild, uncivilized Missouri Territory. The formation of the missionary society proved to be providential. In some respects it had its first great opportunity for service in 1833 in connection with the Oregon Territory.

The story of this begins with a letter written by William Walker, a Christian Wyandot Indian, to G. P. Disoway, a New York businessman, about a trip made by some Flathead Indians of the Northwest to St. Louis searching for the white man's God and how to worship him. They journeyed two thousand miles from the Oregon country through "trackless forests and pathless plains, over untrodden mountains, and down unknown rivers." Only one lived to return to his people.

This sole survivor of the trip in a farewell address made before representative citizens of St. Louis told of his disappointment and how with sad heart he would return empty to his people: "I came with one eye partly opened. I go back with both eyes closed. How can I go back blind to my blind people? . . . When I tell my poor blind people in the big council that I did not bring the book, no word will be spoken by our old men or young braves. One by one they will rise up and go out in silence." [8]

This story, with the dramatic utterance as set forth in the letter, was widely published in the church press. Because of it the Methodists and Congregationalists began sending missionaries to the Northwest. When Wilbur Fisk read Walker's letter "it was like fire shut up in his bones" and he immediately sounded a call for volunteers to go beyond the Rocky Mountains. Jason Lee, a Wesleyan University graduate, volunteered to go to Oregon as a missionary to the Flatheads. He was appointed by the New England Conference to the "foreign mission west of the Rocky Mountains."

This mission to the Indians did not prove successful, but the by-product of Lee's work was to open Oregon for settlement and

[8] *Ibid.*, II, 202 ff.

to fix the northwest part of the nation, including the present states of Oregon and Washington. "The early history of the Methodist church [in Oregon] is the history of the first American colonization in that state." [9]

The missionary enterprise gives an example of the statesmanship of early missionary leaders such as Lee. To do his work, Lee called upon the Missionary Society to send Christian farmers, mechanics, and professional men to settle in the new, rich country. Lee proved what the church has been slow in learning, namely, that the indirect, informal approach made in building a Christian civilization must accompany the organized, formal one.

Bancroft writes: "The Methodists have been foremost in propagating their principles by means of schools as the history of Willamette University illustrates. In the new communities these means seem to be necessary to give coherence to effort." [10]

During the 1830's another opportunity came to the Missionary Society when Methodists entered Texas. Texas, until annexed in 1845, was regarded as "foreign." At the session of the General Conference of 1836, news of the liberation of Texas from Mexico was enthusiastically received. Martin Ruter, who had returned to educational work and was then president of Allegheny College, volunteered to go to Texas to establish Methodist work. Many tried to dissuade him, but his one reply was, "heaven is no further from Texas than Pennsylvania." [11] He served Texas only five months. During that time he laid the foundations of The Methodist Church in that state.

Wherever early Methodist missionary efforts were started, they opened the way for a stable, civilized society. The missionaries

[9] H. H. Bancroft, *History of Oregon,* II, 677.

[10] *Ibid.,* p. 678.

[11] John O. Gross, *Martin Ruter: Pioneer in Methodist Education* (Nashville: Board of Education of The Methodist Church, 1956), p. 35.

founded schools, built mills, introduced agriculture, and prepared the way for a permanent civilization. The record left by achievements of the young missionary society is monumental.

A discussion of the missions of the early Methodists should include some of the approaches made to the Negro slaves. These must be considered against the background of conditions which existed in the last part of the eighteenth and early part of the nineteenth centuries. Many Negro slaves had come directly from Africa and were only slightly removed from their primitive customs. Looking at this whole subject through twentieth-century social complications can prevent our getting an adequate appreciation of what the missionary efforts meant then to the enslaved Negro. During his three years in America John Wesley manifested a special concern for them. His commission from the governor of Georgia gave him authority to preach to the white settlers, the Indians, and the Negroes. In his journal he says, "A few steps have been taken toward publishing the glad tidings, both to the African and American heathens." All through his life, Wesley was an uncompromising foe of slavery and an advocate of the Negroes' freedom and spiritual development. His bold denunciations of the evil of buying and selling human beings caused his life to be endangered at Bristol, center of the slave trade. Abolition of slavery in England owes much to Wesley's agitation and to his special influence on Wilberforce, the English statesman who fought for Negro emancipation.

Both of America's first Methodist churches, John Street in New York and Sam's Creek in Maryland, enrolled Negro members. "Aunt Betty," Mrs. Heck's Negro servant, was a charter member of John Street Church. Through the early years of the movement, they were regular attendants at Methodist meetings wherever they were held.

Asbury met Negroes on his first trip to New York. He records that hearing them "sing with cheerful melody their dear Redeemer's praise, affected me much, and made me ready to say, 'Of a truth I perceive God is no respecter of persons.' " [12] He often mentions having Negroes in his congregations. These references are always tender and solicitous. In the first Sunday school founded on this continent by Asbury, there were both Negro and white scholars.

When the Missionary Society was formed in 1819, William Capers was one of its members. Under his leadership "the Methodist mission to the slaves" was started in 1829. This in time involved the labors of hundreds of the most capable ministers of the Methodist Church in the Southern states. It has been estimated that at least two thirds of the missionary collections made in the Southern states between 1829 and 1844 were expended for this work.[13] This work was not easy since slaves were generally property of non-Methodists. But the mission among the slaves prospered. Someone said that it won "a larger number of practically heathen converts than all missionary societies had gathered upon all the fields of the heathen world." This work, without question, helped prepare the way for the Negro to take his place as a free person. In 1862 there were more than 200,000 Negro members of Methodist churches in the Southern states.

This upsurge of missionary passion for the salvation of Negroes in America was the indirect cause for Methodists' sending their first foreign missionary. The evangelization of Negroes was given added impetus when the new republic of Liberia was set up. Here manumitted slaves had a chance to build a nation of their own. The American Colonization Society expected

[12] *Journal and Letters*, I, 9.
[13] T. L. Williams, "The Methodist Mission to the Slaves" (Unpublished Doctor's dissertation, June, 1945).

Liberia to be the beachhead from which Christian Negroes would push for the conversion of Africans to Christianity.

Melville B. Cox, who went to Liberia, became America's first foreign missionary. In view of today's qualifications for foreign service he should not have been allowed to go; he was ill with tuberculosis. He lived only five months in that country. However, he went with no apprehensions about his condition. He intended to do quickly all that he was able. This was considerable, for hardly will one find more accomplishments to attribute to a dying man. His epitaph, written by himself, "Let a thousand fall before Africa be given up," furnished the rallying cry for many of the first foreign missionary endeavors. By 1844, the mission had extended its work beyond the boundaries of the original station.

There was deeply rooted in the Methodist people the desire to share the benefits of the gospel with people everywhere. Later, as the church matured, this desire sparked one of the greatest missionary movements since Pentecost. The advance came through women's missionary societies and the accelerated efforts of the mission boards. The first years of the life of Methodism show that it did not preach an isolated, introspective religion. Its basic aim was nothing less than the conquest of the whole world for our Lord.

CHAPTER IX

The Methodist
Church and Education

NO SKETCH OF THE HISTORY OF EDUCATION IN THE METH-
odist Church in the United States can be written without some
reference to John Wesley. While he is often remembered as a
great evangelist, Wesley was one of the greatest educators of
eighteenth-century England. In the history of English education, he must be listed high among the pioneers who created a
concern for education of the masses. Illiteracy in eighteenth-
century Great Britain has been estimated to be as high as 80
per cent. A notable by-product of the Methodist movement was
an aroused interest throughout England in making educational
opportunities available to all people.

Wesley was devoted to sound learning. Readily accepting the
disciplines needed for his personal intellectual growth, Wesley
read continually. While a student at Oxford, he read as he
walked. As an itinerant, he read on horseback. In later life, when
age required him to use a chaise, he had bookshelves in it. Some
of the books left from his library, now at Kingswood School,
Bath, England, include Benjamin Franklin's study on electricity,
Isaac Newton's "Transactions of the Royal Society" and John
Ray's work on the harmony of science and religion in "an age
of very rapid advance in both." Wesley's reading covered
varied areas of scholarship—science, theology, medicine, education, philosophy, and literature.

Kingswood College, Methodism's first venture in education and the model for the first Methodist school in America, was started in 1748 by John Wesley. Its history reflects the high standard that Wesley cherished for Methodist education.

Early Methodists who migrated from England to America brought with them Wesley's conviction about the necessity of education for the maturing of the new converts. At the Christmas Conference in 1784 when the Methodist Episcopal Church was formed, the delegates voted to establish a college. Yet we know the project had been in Asbury's thinking as early as 1780.

John Dickins talked with Asbury about the school in the spring of 1780. After this conversation, Asbury was "absorbed in the idea and presented it everywhere he went." When he and Thomas Coke met in Delaware to prepare plans for the organization of the Methodist movement in America, it was agreed that the need for an educational institution would be presented to the conference. Between the time of Asbury and Coke's meeting at Barrett's Chapel and the Christmas Conference, the leaders discussed the school both privately and publicly with Methodists. When the conference met, about five thousand dollars had been raised in gifts and collections. Whatever may be said about Cokesbury's misfortunes, it must not be regarded as an impromptu action. It was an undertaking that had been given consideration for several years.

It is also likely that there had been some communications with Wesley about plans for a school. At any rate, Wesley did name the president, the Rev. Mr. Heath, a clergyman in the Anglican Church and a former master of a grammar school in England. Cokesbury's first faculty consisted of Heath and two unmarried assistants, Patrick M'Closky, a "well-educated Irishman," and Freeman Marsh, a Quaker.

Cokesbury was a miniature Kingswood. In fact, Asbury referred to it as "our Kingswood." Asbury took most of the ideas for the curriculum from Wesley's plan for Kingswood. He included some of Wesley's educational notions which Fitchett charitably called Wesley's "odd opinions." While both Wesley and Asbury knew books, they did not understand boys. This fact is illustrated in the famous Kingswood rule concerning play: "The students shall be indulged with nothing which the world calls *play*. Let this rule be observed with the strictest nicety; for those who play when they are young will play when they are old." [1] Southey calls this a "sour German proverb" brought back from the Moravians and notes that Wesley had forgotten the sensible English one which tells us by what kind of discipline Jack may be made a dull boy. [2]

Cokesbury College was located at Abingdon, Maryland, about twenty-five miles north of Baltimore. The building was erected from money given by early Methodists and other interested friends. George Washington passed by the college on his frequent trips from Mount Vernon north. Washington may have been a contributor, for a printed letter addressed to Cokesbury's "annual subscribers" has been found among his papers. The college opened December 6, 1787, with twenty-five students. The student body was made up of orphans, the children of traveling preachers, and of the friends of Methodists. Cokesbury was destroyed in 1795 by a fire thought to have been the work of an arsonist.

When Asbury heard of the fire, he made this entry in his *Journal:*

A sacrifice of £10,000 in about ten years! . . . Its enemies may rejoice, and its friends need not mourn. Would any man give me

[1] John O. Gross, *Cokesbury College* (Nashville: Parthenon Press), p. 31.
[2] Southey, *op. cit.*, II, 52.

£10,000 per year to do and suffer again what I have done for that house, I would not do it. The Lord called not Mr. Whitefield nor the Methodists to build colleges. I wished only for schools—Doctor Coke wanted a college. I feel distressed at the loss of the library.[3]

As the entry shows, Asbury did not believe that American Methodists were ready for a college. He did want each conference to have an academy. He personally led in organizing such schools in Virginia, North Carolina, South Carolina, Kentucky, and Georgia.

Nathan Bangs has intimated that Asbury did not value education. While Bangs was a contemporary of Asbury and doubtless had some reason for the statement, it is difficult to reconcile with the record Asbury left. Asbury gave meticulous care to the varied needs of Cokesbury. Once in Baltimore he went from house to house through snow and cold soliciting for the school. The total amount that he raised for this school in the ten years of its existence has been estimated to be between $75,000 and $100,000.

From the pen of another historian, Frederick W. Briggs, we have a different view of Asbury's attitude toward education:

He believed that where the gospel was effectual it would give freedom and stimulus to the intellectual faculties and that these, as devoted and energized by the gospel, would conduce by their action to the more complete accomplishment of its great end. He thought of education as the gift of a new power; and was anxious that this power should be used under the guidance of Christian principles and of a sense of responsibility, not only for the good of the person in whose individual mind it had been created, but for the benefit of the world.

This quotation should help us understand the Methodist ap-

[3] *Journal and Letters*, II, 75.

proach to education. The first Methodist college was not started for sectarian purposes. Neither was it to serve Methodism as a promotional aid. Here at the source of the educational enterprise Methodists adapted an educational principle which has continued through the years. They expected their schools to render a wide service to the nation as well as to Methodism's own household.

The enrollment of Cokesbury perhaps never exceeded two hundred students during its whole life. Yet two Cokesbury students served their states as United States Senators—Charles Tate from Georgia and Samuel White from Delaware. Another, Valentine Cook, crossed the Alleghenies and became one of the most effective members of the Western Conference.

None of the schools which Asbury started survived. All the efforts were serious and earnest, but the Methodist constituency was not ready for an educational program. Early American Methodists came for the most part from the underprivileged classes. They were the "unlettered, forgotten men and women of their time." They did not have college graduates within their fellowship. A permanent educational program had to wait, therefore, until the church itself had developed from its own constituency leaders qualified to direct it.

These began to emerge at an earlier date than could be normally expected. As the young church moved forward, its people advanced educationally and socially at a rapid rate and young leaders emerged in keeping with this improved status. Judged by any standards these young men were extraordinary persons. Among them was Wilbur Fisk, the first American Methodist to graduate from college, and the first president of Wesleyan University; Martin Ruter, a self-educated man who became a productive scholar and able administrator; John Emory, a man of superior scholarship who assisted The Methodist Church in founding Wesleyan University, the transferring of Dickinson College to the Methodist Church, and the founding of New York University; and Stephen Olin, the first president of Randolph-Macon College.

These men believed Methodism should assume its part in educating men to serve the new nation. John Emory held that if society was to have in it the ideals preached by the church, Methodism must place within the reach of the people the pleasures and profits of learning. Stephen Olin believed that without "due intermixture with the rich and influential" the church could not fulfill its destiny. "Nothing can save us," he declared, "but an able ministry and this cannot be had but through education." [4]

In many ways Martin Ruter was the forerunner of the modern Methodist educational program and its acknowledged leader during the first third of the nineteenth century. Ruter became the principal of Newmarket Academy, the first school in New England. He was the moving spirit behind the organization and one of the largest contributors. His plans for it were too ambitious for his day; he envisioned at Newmarket a full-grown college, with law, theological, and medical schools. (Everett O. Fisk saw in Boston University the fulfillment of Ruter's dream.) [5] Like several other Methodist schools, the location of this school was poorly chosen. Yet to this small place may be traced the inspiration for the founding of Wesleyan University in Connecticut.

At the General Conference in 1820, Ruter was a member of the committee on education. A report of this committee recommended that each annual conference "establish as soon as practicable, literary institutions under their control, in such way and

[4] *Bulletin of Randolph-Macon College* (September, 1956).
[5] *Zion's Herald* (December 10, 1924).

manner as they may think proper." The same General Conference permitted Methodist bishops to appoint traveling preachers as officers and teachers in colleges. Through these two actions, the Methodist Episcopal Church began an era of educational work which was in time to make it a potent factor in the development of Christian higher education in America.

It is significant that the Methodists began to take their educational responsibilities most seriously in the so-called "era of the common man." Andrew Jackson was elected President of the United States in 1828. His election, some students of history say, gave new impetus to the movements to make education accessible to all people. Church colleges aimed "to reduce the charges of education to the lowest possible amount." Augusta College in Kentucky, the first school founded after the 1820 General Conference, was "for the benefit of youth of every class of citizens." This school obtained a charter from the state of Kentucky in 1822. Located at Augusta, Kentucky, on the Ohio River, "the great highway of the new west," it drew many students from the North and the far South. In a published advertisement the trustees expressed the hope that they would be able to raise adequate funds for its support in order to have "all tuition gratis." [6] Martin Ruter became its president in 1828. During his administration the first persons with bachelor's degrees were graduated from a Methodist college.

Randolph-Macon College, which was projected in 1830 by Virginia Methodists, aimed to provide a liberal and finished education for a sum not exceeding one hundred dollars per year for board, room, and tuition. This school, chartered in 1830, has the distinction of being the oldest permanent college connected with The Methodist Church. Wesleyan University was chartered in 1831 and began classes in October of that year. Dickinson

---

[6] William H. Rankins, *Augusta College* (Roberts Printing Company), p. 22.

College, named for John and Mary Dickinson, was chartered in 1783 under the auspices of the Presbyterian Church. Faced with financial difficulties, Dickinson came under the sponsorship of the Methodist Episcopal Church in 1833, after the Philadelphia and Baltimore conferences arranged to assume responsibility.

Allegheny, another college related to The Methodist Church, dates its beginning beyond its Methodist connection in 1833. It, too, was of Presbyterian lineage, having been founded in 1815 by Timothy Alden, a descendent of the John Alden family. Here again we meet the name of Martin Ruter. When the Pittsburgh Conference assumed responsibility for Allegheny College, it persuaded Martin Ruter, who had just come to the pastorate of Smithfield Church, Pittsburgh, from Augusta, Kentucky, to accept the presidency.

McKendree College began in 1828 as a Methodist seminary at Lebanon, Illinois. In 1830 the name was changed to McKendree College in honor of Bishop McKendree, its largest benefactor, who gave it 480 acres of unimproved land. The charter for McKendree College was granted in 1834. In 1836 it had three professors, all of whom were graduates of Wesleyan University. Its first class of seven "talented young men were admitted to the Baccalaureate" in 1841.

Other schools founded before 1830 include an academy at Cazenovia, New York, Maine Wesleyan Seminary, and Genesee Wesleyan Seminary.

One hundred and thirty-three permanent colleges were established by the various churches in the United States between 1830 and 1861. Of these colleges, thirty-two were founded by the Methodist Church. Some of these now are listed among the truly great educational institutions of the nation.

It was not long after the beginnings of the first Methodist institutions that their graduates began to exercise a constructive influence in American life. Several graduates and former students of Methodist institutions founded some of our nation's best-known educational institutions. Among these were John G. Fee of Augusta College, founder of Berea College, Berea, Kentucky; Holland N. McTyeire of Randolph-Macon College, founder of Vanderbilt University; General Fisk of Albion College, founder of Fisk University; Leland Stanford of Cazenovia Seminary, founder of Leland Stanford University. Graduates of Methodist institutions have been indispensable factors in the efforts of The Methodist Church to carry on God's work.

The charters which were granted to the first Methodist colleges are notable for their freedom from narrow sectarianism. Students were welcomed at these schools irrespective of political or religious affiliations. All were founded in harmony with the motto chosen by Wesley for the Kingswood School: *In Gloriam Dei Optimi Maximi In Usum Ecclesiae Et Republicae.* (To the glory of the most high God in the service of the church and state.) Through the years the Methodist colleges have seemed to many to be strange paradoxes—institutions which have given the search for knowledge full freedom in a Christian but nonsectarian atmosphere. The record shows that Methodist institutions have been sound educational instruments. This is inherent in the tradition.

The Methodist Church was slower in getting a program for theological education under way than most of the other churches. It wanted its ministers to rise from the ranks and opposed what was called a "man-made ministry." Ministers called by God, not man, would better understand the needs of the common people. Peter Cartwright said that if God wanted learned men in the ministry, it would be easy for him "to take a learned sinner, and as Saul of Tarsus, shake him over hell, then knock the shades from his eyes, and without any previous theological training send him straightway to preach his gospel." [7] This is reflected in the attitude that Cartwright and other pioneers had toward the trained ministers who came from Eastern universities to the new West.

However, pioneers working under great handicaps continued to insist upon the importance of Methodism's having schools for its ministers. The first such school to come into existence was at Newmarket, New Hampshire, in 1843. This school later was moved to Boston where it became the School of Theology of Boston University. Garrett Biblical Institute at Evanston, Illinois, followed. The great prophet for theological education in the Methodist Church was John Dempster, a man who in one way or another touched the beginnings of the three oldest of Methodism's theological schools—Boston University, Drew, and Garrett. He is also credited with the founding of the Methodist Theological School in Buenos Aires, Argentina. The first theological school in the Methodist Episcopal Church, South, was the Divinity School of Vanderbilt University. This opened in September, 1875.[8]

A study of Methodist education would not be complete without some mention of the educational efforts directly associated with parish churches. Wesley started the first Sunday school on the American continent at Savannah, Georgia, in 1737. Later during his ministry in England, Wesley encouraged the growth and development of Sunday schools. He predicted in his *Journal,* July 18, 1784, that Sunday schools would "become nurseries for Christians."

[7] The Methodist Ministry 1959 (Report of the Department of Ministerial Education, D-1, Board of Education).

[8] Bard Thompson, *Vanderbilt Divinity School* (Nashville: Vanderbilt University Press, 1958).

Bishop Francis Asbury established in 1783 the first Sunday school in the United States at the home of Thomas Crenshaw in Hanover County, Virginia. At the time of the organization of the Methodist Episcopal Church in 1784, the conference members were told that where there were ten children whose parents were in a society, to meet them at least one hour each week. "Let us labor as the heart and soul of one man to establish Sunday schools in or near the places of public worship," was a declaration of that conference.

Despite this earnest exhortation, the Sunday school did not have a warm reception in many parts of the nation. Teaching in the church was opposed as sinful. The story of the difficulty of planting the first Sunday school in Nashville in 1820 probably could be duplicated in other cities. It was conducted in a dilapidated house with no windows. The founder, a Mrs. Grundy, said that she and her associates were called "Sabbathbreakers" and it said of them that they "deserved punishment as disturbers of the peace." When winter came, they asked for permission to remove the school to the basement of a church, but were refused. In order to be sure there would be no trespassing McKendree Church put this notice on its door: "No desecration of the holy Sabbath, by teaching on the Sabbath in this church." [9]

The Methodist Sunday School Union was organized in 1827 for the purpose of promoting interest in the movement throughout the entire church. From this time, the program of religious training of children grew in importance. The vitality of the church and the growth of the Sunday school were closely related.

In spite of all the work done in education since the founding of our church, often there has been a readiness on the part of

[9] Cullen T. Carter, *History of the Tennessee Conference* (1948), p. 70.

some church people to take a hostile or indifferent attitude toward Christian education. Efforts to keep the public informed on the importance of sound education must continue to be a responsibility of The Methodist Church. It has opposed through the years anti-intellectual sentiments which have deprecated scholastic achievements and questioned the value of educated people in society. At its best, The Methodist Church through the years has been the enemy of ignorance, prejudice, and complacency.

CHAPTER X

Our Methodist Heritage

IN 1786, WESLEY ASKED, "HOW IS IT POSSIBLE THAT METH-odism . . . the religion of the heart though it flourishes now as a green bay tree should continue?" He foresaw that the gospel which had been so effectively mediated to his people would move them upward, and they in time would become prosperous and influential. Would they then be able to keep the fires of the Spirit burning, or would they settle down and be content to have a formal religion?

To his question, Wesley replied: "There is one way and there is no other under heaven. If those who gain all they can and save all they can will likewise give all they can, then the more they gain the more they will grow in grace and the more treasure they will lay up in heaven."

Without trying to deal with the matter of stewardship raised here, we do note that Wesley was thinking of the persons who are in grace. These practices, therefore, would contribute to their continued growth. Here is implied the importance of keeping alive in the person a living faith.

John Wesley was an authority on matters pertaining to religious experience. He himself had been transformed by a personal experience at Aldersgate. For more than fifty years after that he studied religion in the lives of the people to whom he ministered. This may be seen by a study of the letters he wrote. He reached some conclusions as a result of his persistent studies and evaluations. These convictions were based not upon the experience of one person but upon thousands. His formula to keep Methodism alive is found in a statement quoted by Hildebrandt in *Christianity According to the Wesleys:* "Preach our doctrine, inculcate experience, urge practice, enforce discipline." [1]

This line gives the secret of Methodism's phenomenal success, in both England and America. From the time of the planting of Methodism in American soil, it grew until it is now listed as the largest Protestant denomination in the United States. This growth was no accident; it was a calculated result based upon certain convictions. These will be briefly reviewed here.

Theology for Methodist preachers has furnished the intellectual framework for mediating the gospel of Jesus Christ. It was not an elective but a serious part of their equipment. In fact, as Colin Williams says, "Methodism represented in her origins a revival of theology as well as a revival of life, and the former was inseparable from the latter." [2] It is a fact of church history that religious awakenings have been associated with the discovery or rediscovery of some great truths. Once when a theologian of our day was asked if present religious interest was evidence of a revival, he said it was not. He insisted that a revival will come only when some great religious verity grips the people. This was true of the beginnings of Methodism. Its theology was intimately connected with its growth.

Theology for our Methodist fathers was relevant and direct. In general it stood over against the prevailing Calvinism. It accepted without question what Wesley called the common fundamentals of Christianity. These were found in the Articles of Religion adopted by the Christmas Conference and came

---

[1] Colin W. Williams, *John Wesley's Theology Today* (Nashville: Abingdon Press, 1959), p. 36.
[2] *Ibid.,* p. 5.

with one exception—the one which deals with civil rulers—from the Thirty-Nine Articles of Religion of the Church of England. Other doctrinal standards set up for early Methodist preachers included fifty-three of Wesley's sermons and his notes on the New Testament. The preachers at the Christmas Conference pledged themselves to "preach the doctrines taught [in] the sermons and the notes on the New Testament."

If someone had asked a Methodist preacher of Asbury's day for a summary of his theology, he could have used Wesley's own words: "Our main doctrines, which include all the rest, are three—that of repentance, of faith, and of holiness. The first of these we account as it were the porch of religion; the next the door; the third religion itself." While we recognize that there was nothing original here, we do know that Wesley breathed new life into a pale and colorless theology that lacked meaning and power.

Methodist preachers proclaimed that man was corrupt and sinful. Yet he was not left helpless. Through repentance he could come to the "porch of religion." There through faith in Christ, he could be delivered from his sins and made a child of God. Sin, to Wesley, was universal and real. It was, to use his own words, "the baleful source of affliction" and its "flood of miseries . . . overwhelms not only single persons, but whole families, towns, cities, and kingdoms." [3] But Wesley's interpretation of sin never stood in isolation. Methodist preachers, taught to interpret man's sinfulness in the light of God's universal love for sinners, aimed to draw from them a creative response to God's regenerating grace. This was the nature of the Methodist evangel which brought stability and character to the moving frontier.

[3] Henry Carter, *The Methodist Heritage* (Nashville: Abingdon Press, 1951), p. 165.

Wesley's third tenet, holiness, follows the regenerated life. Methodist teaching, says Eric W. Baker in his *The Faith of a Methodist*, stressed God's enabling grace, a theological corollary of regenerating grace. "Not only forgiveness but goodness is the gift of God through Jesus Christ. . . . The truth is that goodness, like forgiveness, is something we can neither earn nor buy, neither deserve nor acquire, by any effort of our own. It is the gift of God through Jesus Christ." [4]

The late George Croft Cell held that the uniting of the Protestant doctrine of justification by faith with the Catholic idea of holiness or Christian perfection was one of Wesley's most significant contributions. Alexander Knox, a contemporary of Wesley, said: "Never, elsewhere, except in the apostles themselves and in the sacred books they have left, were the true foundation and the sublime superstructure of Christianity so effectively united."

Benjamin Hellier, a nineteenth-century Methodist theologian, gave this interpretation of the doctrine of sanctification:

Entire sanctification means the sanctification of everything. The sanctification, for example, of the daily work; that is, doing it to the Lord, and, therefore doing it as well as we can. If a ploughman be entirely sanctified, he will plough a straight furrow—or at least try his best to do so. If he be a mason, he will put no bad work into his walls; if a doctor, he will care more about curing his patients than about getting large fees; if he be a minister of religion, he will strive to serve the people of his charge to the utmost of his ability. . . . Entire sanctification means dedicating all our property to God. When Christians ask themselves, How much of my money shall I devote to religious purposes? they do not consider rightly. There ought to be no question of "how much"; all must be devoted to God. . . . Entire

---

[4] Nashville: Abingdon Press, 1958, p. 28.

sanctification means simply this: spending all our time in the Lord's service; making our religion our life, our life our religion.[5]

This doctrine fell into disrepute when it was carried to fantastic extremes by holiness sects. Specialists assumed a proprietary right upon the doctrine. Wesley would not call a man a Methodist who placed the whole stress of religion on any one part of it.[6] Often the people who professed holiness developed a sort of irritating "piosity." In the early part of this century, a line of cleavage divided many local churches and annual conferences between the "holiness" and "antiholiness" groups. In fairness to many who adhered to this Wesleyan belief, we cite the tribute paid by the late Umphrey Lee: "One must realize that there have been some beautiful and humble characters which have adorned this doctrine of Christian perfection. One can only pay tribute to those who quietly and with no spiritual pride have believed that they have reached this stage of perfect love." [7]

The doctrine of assurance or the witness of the spirit may be cited as a specific contribution of Methodism. According to Wesley, this was "the inward impression on the soul whereby the Spirit of God immediately and directly witnesses to my spirit that I am a child of God." This certitude, Wesley held, "was a common privilege for all Christians." [8] Wesley's converts who testified to this consciousness met violent opposition. Once at a meeting, a constable arrested one who had been "eminent for cursing, swearing and all kinds of wickedness." Those characteristics had passed away, however, and the man's life was now exemplary. When Wesley asked the objection, he said, "Why the man is well enough in other things; but his impu-

[5] *Ibid.,* p. 31 ff.
[6] Wesley, *Works,* VIII, 341.
[7] Lee, *Our Fathers and Us,* p. 73.
[8] *Letters,* V, 358-59.

dence the gentleman cannot bear. Why, sir, he says he *knows* his sins are forgiven." Without question, the preaching of the witness of the spirit added great force to the Methodist revival. Methodist preachers not only proclaimed the forgiveness of sin. They held that men would *know* that their sins were forgiven.

The simple propositions of the itinerants' theology have grown into many books and some elaborate tomes which call for profound thinking and study. Today's danger is not in not having a theology that is intellectually respectable; it is in stopping there. One noted theologian remarked that his interest in theology was purely intellectual and that he had no concern for its emotional or practical connotations. If Wesley had held this attitude, there would never have been a Methodist awakening. Intellectual appreciation of our beliefs when held in an abstract, detached manner deadens the church's evangelistic mission.

The issue is not anti-intellectualism. The church needs scholars who are able to reach beyond the surface, but, in the transfer of knowledge, redemptive aims should not be made secondary to intellectual interests.

Methodism, some like to say, "is long on organization but short on theology." This charge may grow out of Methodism's genius in blending practical concerns with scholarly disciplines. Certainly Wesley cannot be accused of indifference to theological truth. He was quick to rebuke bad doctrine. On the other hand, when he used such plain language as, "We know no gospel without salvation from sin," he was accused of lacking scholarship.

Since scholarship is often associated with the abstract, the practical approaches of Methodists seeking results have operated against their reputation for depth. But Methodists should not underestimate their church's contribution to either the body of knowledge or the furthering of God's work. Wesley gave large liberties and said that "Methodists . . . do not insist on your holding this or that opinion; but they think and let think." [9] Methodism was not raised up solely to cultivate a series of impliable orthodox opinions. Its mission was to hold fast the essentials of the faith and to preach the will of God. This called for the application of profound truths to the problems of living. Wesley did not ignore speculative matters, but he held that the mastering of the abstract was basic to sharing in God's redemptive work. His passionate concern for the redemption of persons obviously meant that his theological emphasis would be upon the saving power of Christ. Therefore, his doctrinal standards were reflected not by his sermons on speculative issues but by ones on biblical and experiential Christianity.

The theology of early Methodism was set to music by Charles Wesley. Converts, many of whom could not read, learned the hymns of Charles and John Wesley. These gave to unlearned men and women a theology which molded their thoughts and actions. There is not a doctrine of The Methodist Church that has not been trenchantly expressed in one or more hymns. Teaching through music, our American forebears discovered, was one of the most effective forms of pedagogy.

The Methodist hymnal compiled by John Wesley became in time, Bernard Manning has said, "a treasury for the expression of every state of mind and every condition of the soul." [10] He says it ranks in Christian literature with the Psalms and the Book of Common Prayer.

Methodist theology, however, would never have stirred people if it had not been associated with powerful preaching. The

[9] *Journal*, VII, 389.
[10] *The Hymns of Wesley and Watts* (London: The Epworth Press, 1942), p. 13.

great revival which Wesley led was a preaching movement. It was, as one writer has said, Wesley's "supreme instrument." The early Methodist chapels were designated by Wesley as preaching houses. Wesley for fifty years preached an average of over eight hundred sermons annually.

This concern for platform ability inspired efforts for self-improvement in early Methodist lay preachers. Wesley exhorted his preachers to study. He himself took time to teach them. Asbury as a young lay preacher received instruction from Wesley in the "new room" at Bristol. Wesley desired "deep preaching." This, he knew, required wide reading. "Through the foolishness of preaching" the Methodist movement swept England and later the United States.

Whatever we may think about the current neglect of the forms of worship Wesley prepared for the young church in America, we cannot escape the conclusion that they were too formal then for American Methodists. There still remains a saturation point among Methodist people on the amount of ritual they will accept. What they want and expect in the pulpit is a preacher, not a liturgist.

The sort of preaching with which Methodism has been associated may be described as prophetic. It must not be confused with entertaining speeches full of amusing anecdotes. Wesley himself did use stories in his sermons, but they were not ends in themselves. Sir Walter Scott, who heard him preach, remarked, "He told excellent stories." The aim of preaching was for a verdict, not a "hung jury."

Methodist preachers traditionally belong to the order of prophets—not priests. Through the preaching of God-filled men, Methodism advanced across our continent, disturbing the consciences of sinners and creating a climate friendly to eternal moral principles. Mention was made in a previous chapter of the attitude of the Methodist Church toward slavery. The church denounced all evils, but the liquor traffic was from the church's inception vigorously denounced. James Finley said, "I suffered no opportunity to pass that I did not improve in portraying the physical, social, and moral evils resulting from intemperance." [11]

The Methodist minister continues to serve a people who expect the pulpit to be a fulcrum that lifts. So long as there are public and private sins demanding rebukes, wrongs to be righted, and rights to be defended, so long as faltering followers need steadying and inspiring, the pulpit, not the reading desk, will be the throne of the Methodist preacher.

Along with the doctrines, the plan Wesley provided for the care of new converts must be considered. He did not leave spiritual nurture and growth to chance.

Wesley did not set up for admission into his society any doctrinal tests. Neither did he hold rigidly to any particular form of worship or manner of administering the sacraments. His only condition was: "Is thy heart . . . right as my heart is with thy heart? If it be, give me thine hand." [12] The basic requirement was "a desire to save their souls." Let no one conclude that this liberality meant indifference to discipline for growth, however. After the convert had repudiated the old way, he had to be prepared to walk in newness of life. If the house from which the unclean spirit had been cast out was left empty, evil in multiplied forms re-entered "and the last state of that man becometh worse than the first." Wesley recognized this. He provided for the spiritual growth of the new converts through fellowship.

Bishop McConnell said that Wesley did succeed in starting a fire of new interest in Christianity by applying the torch

---

[11] *Autobiography* (New York: Eaton & Mains, 1853), pp. 250-51.
[12] Wesley, *Letters*, II, 9.

at the bottom of the social heap. Most of his converts had no previous religious background. They were the social outcasts— the neglected men and women of their day. The class meetings furnished Wesley the instrument needed to conserve the results of the religious awakening.

In order to develop the maturity in his followers which would make them intelligent, aggressive Christians, Wesley placed them in small groups. The absolute necessity of this plan, John Simon says, was a "fixed idea" with Wesley. This strong conviction doubtless came out of his own personal benefits from meeting with small groups. Wesley was a product of two, the Holy Club at Oxford and the Moravian Society in London.

Canon E. R. Wickman of Sheffield, England, gives this estimate of their value:

The class meetings became the strong ground-structure of the Methodist Societies, accomplishing ends that were never envisaged— not only religious and pastoral but also creating vital centers of responsible community life. They produced an active and articulate laity such as no other denomination has produced, not only within the connexion but in secular society.[13]

Bishop F. Gerald Ensley in an address at the Eighth Ecumenical Methodist Conference stressed the indispensable place that the small groups have in the cultivation of the religious life. He said:

Christianity cannot be promoted effectively without small societies supplementing the regular services of the Church where opportunities are given for intimate spiritual fellowship. For Wesley there could not be a vital body of Christ without living cells of comradeship, little clusters of serious-minded individuals who prayed, sang, searched the

[13] *Church and People in an Industrial City.*

Scriptures, and edified each other by religious conversation. . . . While Wesley believed in the power of preaching to awaken and to convert, he looked to the "two or three gathered together" as the real growing edge of Christian discipline and discipleship.[14]

The Methodist class meeting, called Methodism's "one striking and original contribution to the institutions of the church," followed a plan used by the early church. In the first-century church, Christians learned in small groups the nature of the new faith and received instruction to make them intelligent followers of Christ. Modern educators have discovered the dynamism latent in group relationships and the interaction of individuals within the groups.

The class meetings belong to history and do not fit into the mood and temper of our day. Some older Methodists may recall how meaningless and sterile the repeated testimonies could become. But growth in Christian living calls for some plan for giving persons training in the faith. When our churches, with their large and small memberships, have in them dynamic fellowship centers paralleling the class meetings, Christianity will be better prepared to meet the challenge of our century.

Methodists have had a leading place among Protestant groups in their concern for training children in religion. This, too, is a part of the Wesleyan heritage. In a century which was indifferent to the values in childhood and noted for its cruel and inhuman treatment of children, Wesley thought of children as worthy of salvation. His ideas about the training of children had been formed in the Epworth household by observing the practices followed by his mother, Susannah Wesley. Wesley's background doubtless accounts for some of his unreasonable

---

[14] *Proceedings of the Eighth Ecumenical Methodist Conference* (London: The Epworth Press, 1951), p. 114. Used by permission.

and impractical notions, but they should not be allowed to discredit his aims.

Wesley believed that a genuine and meaningful Christian life was possible for children. His views are summarized as follows:

The goal of all work with children at home, in the schools and in the Methodist societies is to make them pious, to lead to personal religion and to insure salvation. It is not merely to bring them up so that they do no harm and abstain from outward sin, nor to get them accustomed to the use of the means of grace, saying their prayers, reading good books and the like, nor is it to train them in right opinions. The purpose of religious education is to instill in children true religion, holiness, and the love of God and mankind and to train them in the image of God.[15]

Wesley prepared many tracts for the instruction of children. These contained what he called the "plainest and most useful portions of the Scriptures." Teachers were enjoined to carefully "teach these deep things of God," but not by rote and memorization. The goal of his educational plan was to help children "understand every single sentence that they read." He deplored parroting memory verses in robot fashion.

All Wesley's educational aims were grounded in his theology. He believed that children were outside the plan of redemption as a result of Adam's fall and needed God. Religious training was made an integral part of Christian home life. Unless Methodist parents assumed an obligation to create in their children a desire for salvation, they abetted atheism. It was not consistent with their Christian profession to let days go by without mentioning God to their children or even alluding to God, while they talked on every other conceivable subject.

[15] Ibid.

At the beginning of the Methodist movement concern for the religious instruction of the rising generation became one of the Methodist preachers' responsibilities. Preaching once or twice a week, Wesley held, was only one part of their office. Even preaching as often as once or twice a day offered no excuse from other essential duties. "What avails public preaching alone, though we could preach like angels?"

At the first conference of Methodist preachers in 1744, Wesley charged the preachers to instruct the children in religion. The plan for Christian training as outlined at this conference included responsibility for reviving and guiding family worship, teaching the children in the home, and forming, in the larger societies, societies for children.

The societies for children were the first Methodist efforts for the religious instruction of children. These met an hour each week and used lesson materials which Wesley had prepared. To preachers who objected to this rigid demand for instructing the children because they had no gifts for such work, Wesley gave this answer: "Gift or no gift, you are to do it, else you are not called to be a Methodist preacher."

The educational practices used by Wesley became the pattern for instruction in the United States. One of the first three books distributed by the Book Concern after its organization was on instructing children in religion. The first *Discipline* contained a section on the instruction of children. It was taken from the minutes of conferences Wesley held for Methodist preachers.

From the beginning of his ministry in America, Asbury observed faithfully Wesley's instructions for instructing children. At the Christmas Conference in 1784, the preachers were urged to support Sunday schools. This was an advanced step for religion in the United States. Then Sunday schools were regarded by most of the established churches as a desecration of both the Sabbath and the church. But the Methodists brought Christian education into the church and made it a responsibility of the ministerial office. From this humble beginning there has been developed in The Methodist Church the most advanced program of Christian education this nation knows.

Already attention has been called to the adoption of plans for Cokesbury College at the Christmas Conference. For an assembly which contained only one college graduate—Thomas Coke—it was a daring adventure to take. However, both Thomas Coke and Francis Asbury agreed that the new church could not advance in the nation without schools. While American Methodists were not financially prepared to support their program of higher education, they did believe in its importance. They perhaps saw, even though dimly, that each generation was obligated to prepare leaders to serve the next one. As the Methodist Episcopal Church moved upward socially and educationally, its colleges furnished the leaders to serve on the advanced levels. If the successors of the circuit rider had not been better prepared for their work than their predecessors, many gains previously made would have been endangered. The succeeding years have demonstrated that schools are indispensable to the church.

Another factor accounting for the spread of Methodism was Wesley's use of lay preachers. Wesley never discounted the contribution made by the amateur. He once confessed that he had learned more on his trip to Germany at Herrnhut from a carpenter, Christian David, than from the scholars, including Count Zinzendorf. This man, he noted, had peace of mind in perfect harmony with the divine mind. Wesley's "lay assistants" provided manpower needed for the Methodist revival. Wesley, the dedicated churchman, saw that they functioned as laymen and not professionals. As laymen he expected them to share their experiences with others.

Asbury had begun his work as a local preacher under Wesley. This provided the background that America's first general superintendent needed. He quickly marshalled a body of lay preachers and made them into a mobile force.

Our Methodist heritage is a sacred trust. In our day when denominational differences are deplored, there may be a tendency to treat it lightly. Church union, not divisions, is the goal to be emphasized. We should be grateful for the present deepened fellowship among Protestant churches and the prospects for church union. However, nothing could be more disastrous to the body of Christ than for the Protestant churches to discard the distinctive values developed by their traditions. A failure of The Methodist Church to carry over into the total life of Christendom some of its unique characteristics will shortchange the organization it aims to strengthen. Not only are these important for the building up of our own faith, but they should be held in trust for the Church Universal.

We Methodists do have a character and history that are distinctly our own.

What Ralph Barton Perry said about our nation is equally true of our church:

The chief source of spiritual nourishment for any nation must be in its own past, perpetually rediscovered and renewed. A nation which negates its tradition loses its historic identity and eventually destroys its chief source of spiritual vitality. A nation which merely reaffirms its tradition grows corrupt and stagnant.[16]

Let us, therefore, rejoice in the way God has used our spiritual ancestors in the past and pray that he will give to us the ability to serve the present age as effectively as our forebears served theirs.

[16] *Puritanism and Democracy* (New York: Vanguard Press, 1944), p. 627.

BIBLIOGRAPHY

Autobiography of Peter Cartwright. Nashville: Abingdon Press, 1956.

Baker, Eric. *The Faith of a Methodist.* Nashville: Abingdon Press, 1958.

Bready, J. Wesley. *England Before and After Wesley.* London: Hodder and Stoughton Limited, 1938.

Bushford, James W. The Oregon Missions.

Church, Leslie F. *Knight of the Burning Heart.* Nashville: Abingdon Press, 1953.

Edwards, Maldywn L. *Family Circle.* London: The Epworth Press, 1949.

Fitchett, W. H. *Wesley and His Century.* New York: Eaton & Mains, 1906.

Flint, Charles W. *Charles Wesley and His Colleagues.* Washington, D. C.: Public Affairs Press, 1957.

Garber, Paul N. *Romance of American Methodism.* Greensboro, N. C.: The Piedmont Press, 1931.

Gross, John O. *Martin Ruter: Pioneer in Methodist Education.* Nashville: Board of Education of The Methodist Church, 1956.

_____. *Methodist Beginnings In Higher Education.* Nashville: Board of Education of The Methodist Church, 1959.

Harmon, Nolan B. *Understanding The Methodist Church.* Nashville: Abingdon Press, 1955.

Henry, Stuart C. *George Whitefield: Wayfaring Witness.* Nashville: Abingdon Press, 1957.

Journal and Letters of Francis Asbury. Nashville: Abingdon Press, 1950.

Lee, Umphrey. *John Wesley and Modern Religion.* Nashville: Cokesbury Press, 1936.

_____. *The Lord's Horseman.* Nashville: Abingdon Press, 1954.

_____. *Our Fathers and Us.* Dallas: Southern Methodist University Press, 1958.

Lee, Umphrey, and Sweet, William W. *A Short History of Methodism.* Nashville: Abingdon Press, 1956.

Luccock, Halford E., Hutchinson, Paul, and Goodloe, Robert W. *The Story of Methodism.* Rev. ed. Nashville: Abingdon Press, 1949.

Mathews, H. F. *Methodism and the Education of the People.* London: The Epworth Press, 1949.

McConnell, Francis J. *John Wesley.* Nashville: Abingdon Press, 1939.

Peters, John L. *Christian Perfection and American Methodism.* Nashville: Abingdon Press, 1956.

Sweet, William W. *Methodism in American History.* 2nd ed. Nashville: Abingdon Press, 1954.

—————————. *Religion on the American Frontier.* Vol. IV. Chicago: University of Chicago Press, 1946.

Tees, Francis H. *Beginnings of Methodism in England and in America.* Nashville: The Parthenon Press, 1940.

Tipple, Ezra S. *Francis Asbury: Prophet of the Long Road.* Cincinnati: The Methodist Book Concern, 1916.

Tippy, Worth Marion. *Frontier Bishop.* Nashville: Abingdon Press, 1958.

Whiteley, J. H. *Wesley's England.* London: The Epworth Press, 1938.

Williams, Colin W. *John Wesley's Theology.* Nashville: Abingdon, 1959.

INDEX